OutSell
Yourself®

"Kelly's great insights and strong skills will help anyone improve their track record of sales. Many books have sales techniques. Kelly has sales realities. This book is a game changer for anyone involved in sales."

Kathy Ireland
CEO and Chief Designer, Kathy Ireland Worldwide

"Mr. Morita, the founder of Sony, once told me that 'customer' connotes a relationship built on trust over a long period of time. Kelly shows us the way to grow a customer base for the future. Take advantage of her wisdom."

Frank Maguire
Cofounder of FedEx

"FINALLY, a book that discusses the differences between selling to women and to men! In *OutSell Yourself*, Kelly McCormick shares how and why women buy differently than men and how you can effectively sell better to both. This book is a valuable resource; it's filled with the methods entrepreneurs have been waiting for!"

Tera McHugh
Founder of Association of Women Entrepreneurs

"If you think that this is just another sales book, think again. *OutSell Yourself* shows you a whole new way to sell. Kelly's positive, personal, and conversational style comes screaming out of this book. Whether you're new to business and selling or simply want to increase your skills; you get the tools to be totally ethical and customer focused. This book is the one to buy."

David Cohen
Founder of the Small Business, Big Ideas Show

"I learned valuable sales and marketing strategies while editing Kelly's book. In fact, I used her techniques to land my next major editing/coaching project—my most lucrative contract so far!"

Mary Jo Tate
Editor and Book Coach, Tell Me Your Book

"*OutSell Yourself* is a must read if you want to grow your business. I never enjoyed the old hard sell sales method. Kelly showed me to how move forward into the 21at century and generate sales in a new way."

Janice Smith
Author of *Era of the Rebel: Embracing Your Individuality*

"*Outsell Yourself* completely shifted my way of thinking about the sales process. When it came to selling, I was so caught up in an internal ethics battle that I'd often sabotage myself early on. After reading this brilliantly written book, I have the confidence to master my future sales with ease."

Kristianna Berger
Communications Consultant, KBirdPR

"Outsell Yourself is filled with practical advice that's needed to deal with today's crazy-busy prospects. Kelly shows you strategies you can use to sell without selling. Good stuff!"

Jill Konrath
Author of *SNAP Selling* and *Selling to Big Companies*

OutSell
Yourself

GO FROM **HELLO** TO
SOLD WITH ETHICAL
BUSINESS AND
SALES TECHNIQUES!

Kelly McCormick

Matthew Publishing
Malibu, California

Published by Matthew Publishing

Jacket design: Dunn+Associates
Cover photo: Maria Laxamana
Interior design: Dorie McClelland, Spring Book Design
Editor: Mary Jo Tate

ISBN-13: 978-0-9844637-0-1

Library of Congress Cataloging-in-Publication Data
McCormick, Kelly, 1958-
    OutSell yourself : go from hello to sold with ethical
    business and sales techniques! / Kelly McCormick. — 1st ed.
    p. cm.
    Includes bibliographical references and index.
    ISBN-13: 978-0-9844637-0-1
    ISBN-10: 0-9844637-0-4

    1. Selling. 2. Marketing.   I. Title.
HF5438.25.M33 2010   658.85
            QBI10-600029

Printed in the United States of America
First Edition

To Bob McCormick and Frances McCormick

Your wisdom and guidance have meant more than you'll ever know. I so appreciate that you are my parents!

CONTENTS

INTRODUCTION

OutSell Yourself®—What's It All About?

Do you know anyone who sat in their highchair, shook their rattle, and cried, "50% Off Sale—Buy now or miss out"? Neither do I.

Few people are born knowing how to sell. Many stumble their way through the process. They have the bruises to show and the war stories to tell. You have to wonder whether they even enjoy selling. I doubt it. The reality is that most people don't really like having to sell. Are you one of them? I was . . . until I finally figured out how to offer my services and products in a way that worked for my clients and me. These same methods to sell with ease are here for you.

Discovering the keys to OutSell myself has enabled me to become an international speaker, consultant, and coach. Today I educate others to OutSell themselves. In between working with clients and racking up frequent flyer miles while traveling to speak to audiences, I also write articles for sales and business magazines and industry trade publications. But I'm jumping ahead of myself. Like many people, before I was able to excel when exchanging my solutions for money, I had a lot to learn and many growing pains to endure.

There Must Be a Better Way

By age thirty-five, I had launched three successful businesses, but I hated to sell. Whenever I thought about selling, what came to mind was manipulation and guilt. Persuasion seemed to drive the deal. At the end of the day, I'd walk away feeling like I'd sold a piece of myself just to make a living. Yuck! Owning a business was a dream come true, but to continue to feel the passion for my work, I had to find a way to be myself and still pay the bills.

Sell with a Clear Conscience

Fortunately, a lot has changed. In our virtual, high-tech, low-touch world, buyers yearn to connect with a real person. It's not only okay to be yourself; people expect it. Authenticity, trust, and integrity make up the new sales model. Customers have so many choices that they don't have to put up with anyone who seems insincere, deceptive, or unreliable.

For me this was great news. It made it possible to sell without having to act like a high-pressure salesperson. It's also why I wrote *OutSell Yourself*—to give you the same tools to be able to sell with a clear conscience in any situation. Plus, for well over a decade, clients and audiences have asked me, "Do you have a book with all of this information?" Well, now my conscience is clear about that too. The answer is finally, "Yes, and you're reading it!" So let's keep going.

1

No More Sleepless Nights

Have you ever spent a night tossing and turning as selling concerns swirled in your brain? If so, you're not alone. Many of the professionals who now use my OutSell Yourself techniques used to worry about why a sale might not come together. Many admitted to lying in bed running worst-case sales scenarios through their heads. Instead of sleeping soundly, they stared at the ceiling. Hours were spent strategizing how to respond to endless buying concerns and objections.

By the time morning arrived, they were exhausted and overly anxious. It wasn't difficult for a potential buyer to quickly sense that something was out of whack. Before they knew it, the sales conversation had fallen apart faster than a brick wall propped up with crazy glue. But that changed when they applied the strategies outlined in this book.

Increase Your Sales with Less Effort

Whether you sell products or services, as an entrepreneur or for a company, you can absolutely increase your sales with less effort. Here's the best part: When you OutSell Yourself, you'll never need to use hard-sell techniques to generate long-term success. As a matter of fact, you'll actually learn how to sell without selling. It can be easier than you might imagine. But before we dive into the specific steps in the OutSell Yourself approach, I'll share some of the key principles that have driven my sales success for years. All of these concepts are covered in greater detail throughout the book. However, hearing about them now will give you a context for what you're about to learn, and it will help you to embed the principles into your business practices.

Generate Your Own Success

To increase sales without ever experiencing stress, I researched what it takes to actually think your way to success, on both the subconscious and conscious level. Powerful think-to-succeed techniques, similar to those used by winning Olympic athletes, will set you up to succeed long before you ever meet a client. I know because I've been using the techniques for years. But that wasn't always the case. You will read more about my earlier self-sabotaging behaviors. And you'll learn the same think-to-succeed methods that I've used to turn many careers around almost overnight—mine included. (*Find out more in chapter 2.*)

Attract Your Ideal Client—Oprah Style

As you hone your success, you can also attract your dream clients to you—Oprah style. *The Oprah Winfrey Show* has a huge following of dedicated viewers. People from around the globe tune in regularly to get their daily dose of Oprah. However, this didn't just happen by accident; it happened by design. Once I let you in on how to attract loyal buyers, there will be no turning back . . . that is, if you don't fall into the trap of trying to be a one-size-fits-all seller. (*Find out more in chapters 2 and 3.*)

Be the Expert and Thrive—Generalists Barely Survive

Resisting the temptation to be the Jack-or-Jill-of-all-trades can be tough. After all a sale is a sale—or is it? The answer is yes and no. The downside of trying to be all things to all buyers is that it brands you as a generalist and you'll forever be known as "the person to see if you want generic solutions at rock-bottom prices." On the other hand, an expert offers real solutions that meet real needs. In today's economy, experts thrive while generalists barely survive.

To reinforce your expert status, a well-thought-out chart enables you to build a solid selling plan around your niche market. You will quickly map out how and where to package and promote your products or services to make the best impact with your ideal buyer—at the right price . . . assuming you know what to charge. (*Find out more in chapter 3.*)

Quit Undervaluing Your Worth

When you're not sure of what price or fee to charge, it can be a huge challenge not to panic. It can also throw you into the cycle of working far too hard for the money. To keep you in the flow of prosperity, several methods are here to assist in determining what your expertise, goods, and/or services are truly worth. (*Find out more in chapter 3.*) However, to really stay in the groove, there is another important issue to address head on. It centers on your competition.

Don't Let Your Competition Ruin You

Whether you set your own rates or they are established by a company or distributor, there's a potentially fatal oversight that can haunt you: not knowing what your direct and indirect competitors charge. Without this information, you risk giving away the store.

What if you present your price and the client takes a moment to think things over? Even a second of dead air space can throw a hardened professional into a tizzy. Suddenly, unwarranted discounts or needless slashing of rates appear out of nowhere. Look out! Worse yet, your customer could say, "I can buy it cheaper elsewhere" or "I can hire someone less expensive." How would you know for certain?

To nip this dicey situation in the bud, use my process to ethically find out what your competition charges. Knowing this information can boost your confidence and prepare you for whatever comes your way. (*Find out more in chapter 3.*)

Give Your Buyers What They Really Want

Before you get too deep into the sales process, it's important to understand the top three things that motivate a person to select your products and services. However, most people don't really know what influenced someone to purchase from them.

This explains why a lot of sellers give boring sales presentations, either in person or on the phone. They have a misguided hope that something in the conversation will strike a buying chord. Talk about a colossal waste of time, energy, and self-esteem. It works in your favor to be aware of a customer's true buying motivators. Then you'll never again have to sell to get a sale. (*Find out more in chapter 4.*)

Apply the Sell without Selling Process

Does this sound familiar? "When I first started out in business, I didn't have a clue about how to speak to customers. Often looking at my shoes, I would sputter and stammer as I recited why someone should consider my products and services." If any part of that description caused you to recoil, you're not alone. That was a mini recap of how my selling career began.

Everything is different today. My fake-it-until-you-make-it sales talk has been replaced with an interactive **Discovery Dialogue**. When we've finished speaking, it's clear to me and my client what they really need. It's also obvious that I'm the perfect person for the job. The same results can happen for you.

Use my step-by-step blueprint to have a collaborative sales discussion. It's packed with purposeful questions that quickly build trust and uncover exact needs and budgets. You and your buyer will both appreciate the Sell without Selling process. (*Find out more in chapter 5.*)

Increase Your Sales to Women

Why not increase your sales to the fastest-growing group of consumers? Women! Globally, females spend an estimated nineteen trillion dollars each year. They also make and or influence approximately 80 percent of all buying decisions. However, to see even a fraction of that business, you must know how to sell to a woman.

To adapt your sales approach for this powerful market, we will go on a journey into a woman's world. You'll discover what makes her buying style so distinctive. This includes understanding what she looks for in products, services, and sellers.

Plus, you'll get critical information about how women communicate. You'll know what you need to say to gain a woman's buying trust and to uncover what she's really looking for. In addition, women's unique decision-making style has been demystified for you. This includes setting the record straight on what it takes to get their repeat and referral business. (*Find out more in chapters 4–9.*)

Make Your Buying Point with Men

Men have a distinct buying style too—as many of us have found out the hard way. If you want to capture a man's buying attention, it's important to know why he has turned to you for help. You also need to know what you could innocently say that would have him grab his cell phone to find a different seller. Fortunately all that information is here for you.

In addition, I let you in on what his real goals are when he gets ready to make a purchase for his home or business. Finally, as you prepare to make your recommendations, you'll get the exact words and phrases that line up with his way of thinking. (*Find out more in chapters 4–9.*)

Flush Out the Real Decision Maker

When selling to a couple or committee, have you ever wanted to ask, "Would the real decision maker please stand up?" What about when trying to solicit the opinions of silent buyers? Ever wondered who was really in charge? Well, to take the frustration and guesswork out of the equation, you get the key questions that flush out those with high levels of influence. Soon you'll be shouting, "The sale just got easy again!" (*Find out more in chapter 5.*)

Check In to Move Forward

Who wouldn't want to meet with the buyer who easily volunteers information? Well, that would be every seller I've ever met. That is until the client turns into a person who shares what can seem like endless facts, figures, and buying expectations. Suddenly your head begins to ache from information overload.

To save the day, use my cut-to-the-chase check-in and

clarifying statements. This process makes extra certain that you don't miss any important points or misinterpret anything that your client might say. And the great news is that customers and clients have commented that when they rehear the key things they just stated, they feel "heard," "understood," and "more trusting of the seller." Using check-in statements is what quickly separates the beginners from the pros. (*Find out more in chapter 6.*)

Focus on the Benefits to Sell More

Which would you buy? A stereo equipped with the Quasimodo Static feature? Or the same model described like this: "This stereo has the Quasimodo Static feature *that makes even the fuzziest audio sound crystal clear.*" If I were to wager a bet, my guess would be that you'd pull out your credit card for the crystal-clear sound. And what if you were looking to hire a business coach? Would you sign on with a person whose website only listed the services they offered? Or with a coach whose site also provided details on how their services *could improve your business?* I'd say that the chances are good that you'd pick the coach who could state where and how your business could grow.

Customers and clients may be attracted to the features of what you offer; however, it's the benefits of your products and services that win them over. The majority of sellers I've worked with often confuse features with benefits. Regrettably, if you highlight only the features, you could lose a potential buyer.

Not anymore. I've made it easy to differentiate between the two. Faster than you can say, "Do you want fries with that soda?" you will have amassed an impressive benefit list. This will grab your customer's full buying attention. (*Find out more in chapter 7.*)

Take the Guesswork out of Preparing Proposals and Quotes

It can be a struggle to settle on which selling options to include in your proposals and quotes. As an alternative, I show you how to absolutely do away with any guesswork. You'll know what to say and do so that buyers work with you to determine what will solve their problems.

Yes! You read that correctly. Clients become involved in selecting the best solutions for them—solutions so targeted that they match their exact buying criteria, budget, and anticipated ROI (return on investment). You'll be a big step closer to writing your winning proposal. (*Find out more in chapter 7.*)

Think like a CEO

There's another surefire way to make a great impression with an individual or business. It happens when you think like a corporate decision maker as you put your proposal or quote together. To help with the process, I take you inside a CEO's head and answer their potential buying questions—the ones you may have thought about as well as ones you may not have considered. Then you'll know exactly what to include in your quote and what to avoid.

To further assist you, my user-friendly **4 Steps to a Great Written Proposal** process converts the information into a top-notch written proposal. If you respond to RFPs (requests for proposals), I clarify what it takes to prepare your bang-on response.

When you deliver selling solutions and quotes verbally, my **4 Steps to a Great Face-to-Face Presentation** process makes certain you give any potentially boring face-to-face presentations the heave-ho. These resources make it easy for your proposals and quotes to pass the CEO test. (*Find out more in chapter 7.*)

Avoid Choking When Money's on the Table

If you've ever felt your gag reflex engage when it's time to talk about your prices and fees, you'll love what else is here for you. You get specific communication techniques that take the emotional charge out of discussing money. The potent language makes it possible to swallow what you're about to say and speak at the same time. (*Find out more in chapter 7.*)

Turn Objections into Opportunities

You could come face to face with a customer who voices an objection or concern. Does that mean that you screwed up? Not necessarily. It could be that your client had a lousy buying experience in the past. Then there are industries or particular situations where the same issues always surface. Whatever the reason, your reaction will either move things forward or slam the sales door shut.

To avoid falling into defending, arguing, or neglecting to address the real problem, my nonthreatening responses uncover the true issues. All the while, they demonstrate your respect for the customer. They also keep the conversation moving forward because "no" doesn't always mean no.

You'll be able to respond to price concerns such as "Is this your best price?" "Your fee [price] is too high," "That seems expensive," and "Things have changed. The price is higher than our current budget."

Plus, you'll know how to deal with the biggest red-flag mouthful of them all: "We really like your stuff [products, services, ideas, solutions], but could you drop the price a bit? We're on a tight budget. However, you'll probably get more business [sales, referrals . . .] from this." (*Find out more in chapter 8.*)

Don't Give Up—Keep Yourself Afloat

If you sell within the not-for-profit world, you can meet groups and organizations that have little or no budget. To manage what sometimes seems like endless requests for reduced fees and freebies, use my **Give Back to the Community** policy. It's part of the **Keep Kelly McCormick Afloat** program. You can adapt the policy to use in a variety of situations. My methods have kept lots of vendors' and service providers' heads above water. (*Find out more in chapter 8.*)

Never "Close" a Sale Again

Most sellers choke when it's time to ask, "So are you ready to buy?" They could be rejected. When you OutSell Yourself, you'll never again have to close a sale under any circumstances. In place of closing, there are more genuine statements and questions for you to use. I've put together communication techniques to allow the sale to unfold. You can actually stand back as the customer asks to buy. (*Find out more in chapter 8.*)

Stay in Touch—Without Being Pushy

For the buyer who needs time to compare quotes or to talk to other decision makers, you'll see how to replace dead-end stalker-style follow-ups with far more successful techniques that keep you in the conversation loop. There's no point in risking harassing or annoying your customer, especially when you can work in partnership to wrap up the sale. (*Find out more in chapter 8.*)

Have Your Buyer Introduce You to Your Next Customer

After delivering your product or service, you can continue to build on your success. Sellers who know how to leverage great customer relationships tap into a wealth of business.

Using testimonials and referrals can increase your earnings dramatically. However, if, "Thanks for your business!" has been the final sentence in your sales conversations, you could be losing a fortune in potential income. Instead, why not let your buyer introduce you to your next customer?

Asking for a referral can feel awkward. However, my noninvasive **3-Part After-Sale Inquiry** and **Ask Technique** can make it seem effortless. When you use either technique, prepare to be surprised at the number of clients who will willingly open their wallets and networks to you.

What about testimonials? Are you collecting them? They are extremely valuable. If your buyers are busy decision makers, you'll find out how to offer to write their testimonials—without being pushy.

To make sure that all feedback is powerful, I break down the elements of a great testimonial for you. After you collect the positive feedback, you can refer to my list of the top places and ways to leverage it. Like everything covered in this book, the steps are straightforward and can be put into action with ease. They also keep your database active and growing for years. (*Find out more in chapter 9.*)

Shorten Your Learning Curve

To shorten your learning curve, **Kelly's Keepers** are also placed throughout the book. They are quick summaries of important OutSell Yourself techniques and ideas. You can draw on them as easy memory tools.

Pearls of wisdom from other professionals are woven into the book too, along with some of my more memorable near-miss selling disaster stories. And of course my save-the-day solutions are waiting for you too.

Make It Easy to OutSell Yourself

My goal is to make it easy for you to learn how to OutSell Yourself. To achieve this, each letter in the word **OutSell** represents one of the key selling points. The **OutSell** acronym also makes it simple to look up the exact answers you need, when you need them.

Open Your Mind to Success
Unleash Your Real Value
Tap into Your Client's Buying Motivators
Sell without Selling
Earn the Right to Proceed
Lead with Your Best Solution
Listen to Hear Yes

Simply look for the chapter with the name specific to the selling point and information you want to know more about. Within that chapter, you will find plenty of other methods to OutSell Yourself. And there's even more here for you. To discover how to collect and leverage buyers' testimonials, turn to the final chapter, "Even More Sales, More Often, with Less Effort."

From personal experience, when I use the OutSell Yourself methods, it becomes a whole lot easier to sell with ease and integrity. Using even a few of these insights can speed up the sales cycle and increase your income. And here's the best part: Each skill and exercise has my **Simple-Easy-Doable** stamp all over it. Get ready to OutSell Yourself!

2

Open Your Mind to Success

At age 21, with less than $3,000 in cash and family loans clutched in my hot little hands, my 22-year-old business partner and I opened our first company. With great pride, we nailed the OPEN FOR BUSINESS sign onto the door of our retail sporting goods shop. In less than thirty days, we almost lost our first company too. I'd been officially welcomed into the school of hard knocks!

What I didn't know about selling was laughable, but that was the least of my problems. Fear-based thinking threatened to destroy the business well before my shaky skills would. There was no doubt about it: I was in for a bumpy ride—until I discovered what it took to generate ongoing success. But like many professionals, I had a long way to go before that lesson became clear.

Success or Failure—It's All in Your Mind

Over the years, a nasty reality reared its ugly head. Sellers can develop and even master all of the nonintimidating sales techniques in the world. However, unless they also create an environment for success, they severely compromise their ability to do well or even get ahead. That reality played like the background music in my sales story too. My theme song was: "Times are tough, and it's hard to get a break . . . la la la. . . ."

Three Businesses Later . . .

My fatalistic self-talk, plus far too much self-imposed struggle and effort, laid a shaky foundation for my first two businesses. The retail sporting goods shop, which eventually expanded to two locations, was followed by a four-unit rental property. When I look back, it's a miracle the businesses even got off the ground. The mountain of sabotaging beliefs threatened to bankrupt me several times.

As if I hadn't made my life tough enough, pessimism also seeped into my third business venture. When my career as a speaker, consultant, and coach on sales and marketing got under-way, a typical day at the home office was an exercise in survival. The morning pep talk sounded like this: "There is so much work to do; I don't know how I'll get it all done!" It left me exhausted by 7:30 a.m. Still, I soldiered on. I even told myself I was a real trooper. Wow, was that a joke.

A ringing phone was a welcome distraction . . . until a poten-tial client called. Within seconds, the confident businesswoman vanished and my inner doubts and fears took over. What surfaced from my subconscious mind was a bombardment of success-limiting worries: "I hope I get this job. If not, how will I put food on the table? How will I pay the rent?"

You Are Fired!

Guess what happened? Times got tough, life was hard, and I got what I deserved. The self-defeating thoughts became a self-fulfilling prophecy. As a result, my to-do list remained endless, and for every new client who hired me, at least two prospects went missing in action. As if that weren't stressful enough, paying the bills was a constant struggle. I had reaped what I had sown. My life resembled the slimy pits instead of the fabulous bowl of cherries glorified in greeting cards. Three businesses later, it was clear. The only sane thing to do was *fire* myself. I had to start over.

Move Forward—Once Again

Soon after my pink-slip episode, the time was ripe to check into a thought rehabilitation program. The rehab center was in an ideal location—my brain. Like any good twelve-step program, the first step was to admit that my old behavior didn't work. Once I had hit rock bottom, it was time to move forward. As if by magic, the reasons why some people attracted the perfect customer with ease and sold premium-priced goods and services without doing handstands for the money suddenly appeared. The same life-changing insights and techniques that transformed my career and the careers of others are here for you too.

Life is either a daring adventure or nothing.
HELEN KELLER

Tune To the FM Seller's Success Station

After observing scores of professionals over the years, I know this for sure: It's not luck that determines who achieves great success and who doesn't, as many people would like to believe. It's what sellers *think* that has the most powerful influence on their success.

Manifest the Best Sale of Your Life

What sellers think places them into one of two success categories. You're either a fabulous manifester of great outcomes, or
you're an aimless manifester of random outcomes. People often
ask, "What does it mean to manifest something?" Below you'll
find several different answers, which in my experience all lead to
the same thing.

You manifest an outcome when you:

Have a vision and see it come to fruition

Make something out of nothing

See your dreams come true

MAN·I·FEST

To prove; put beyond doubt or question
MERRIAM–WEBSTER DICTIONARY

It all comes down to this: What you *think* is what you *get*. You
can manifest everything from increasing your income to attract-
ing great clients. When it comes to manifesting, it's only your
thoughts which limit your accomplishments.

What Thoughts Do You Tune In To?

What you think determines who you are and what you achieve.
For example, if you had your own radio sales show, the commen-
tary you wrote would identify you as one of two kinds of sellers:
an FM Seller (Focused Manifester) playing on a FM station or
an AM Seller (Aimless Manifester) playing on an AM station.

Just as the FM and AM bands on a radio will tune you into
different programs, your thoughts tune you into different frequencies. Your thoughts about how easy or how hard it is to

make a sale produce very different energy frequencies. Whatever thought frequency you're tuned into makes it possible to manifest successful outcomes or not. It's that specific.

Whether you think that you can or that you can't,
you are usually right.

HENRY FORD

Focused Manifester

As focused manifesters of successful outcomes, FM Sellers broadcast a top sales producer message. The theme of their show is THINK IT—FEEL IT—SEE IT. FM Sellers tap into high-producing thoughts every time they set personal and professional goals, speak to potential customers, and get ready to let the sale unfold.

Aimless Manifester

AM Sellers, who are aimless manifesters of random outcomes, replay a blast from the past sales program. Their LIFE IS TOUGH—AND THEN—YOU DIE talk show airs daily. AM Sellers complain about everything from slumps in the economy to competitive markets and the sheer volume of traffic—all of which are somehow responsible for their low sales. Talk about a tough gig. If AM Sellers are lucky, they might get a break some day, maybe. If they can even imagine it could be possible.

Do You Need to Change Your Station?

To be an FM Seller and see consistent success, you must take intentional actions. Here's the good news: The process is easier than most people think. Quite simply, it begins when you tune out any thoughts and beliefs that create static and interfere with your success. Then you can turn on communication that makes a real difference.

Tune Out Static Interference

What you say is what you get. There are scientists, physicists, and a host of other equally noteworthy "ists" who state that our thoughts are real and what we think really does matter. Popular culture has also jumped on the thoughts-produce-outcomes bandwagon. A recent Google search revealed 2,670,000 websites related to the topic. Don't worry: You don't have to read all that information to find out what's what. Laid out here are some powerful thoughts for you to consider.

What You Think Is What You Get

Over the years, I was seeing a recurring scenario. Even though my clients used the same OutSell Yourself sales tools, there were some whose sales blew through the roof while others perpetuated a pattern of struggle and effort to make ends meet. So what was up?

As my own career challenges revealed, we lay the foundation to realize consistent success well before we ever meet a client. Those who live in abundance operate from a deep-seated belief that they will make it. The positive language they use to describe their situation, goals, and desired outcomes propels them forward. They let nothing interfere with their success, no matter what. That's just the way it is.

To turn off negative thoughts, you must increase your verbal self-awareness. What that means—and there's no easy way to say this: You need to listen to what comes out of your mouth.

Kelly's Keepers
Your thoughts produce your outcomes.

Tune In Your Verbal Self-Awareness

It takes a high level of verbal self-awareness to think and speak thoughts that fuel your success. However, most people have little to no awareness of what they say. They also have no idea of what they sound like when they talk. You can see it in their eyes.

Can You See Me?

From my side of the consulting table, I've noticed that most people in the traditional North American culture seldom look at a listener when they speak. Instead, they go into their brains, grab hold of their well-worn and well-rehearsed sales stories, and forget to look at the people in front of them. If sellers disconnect from themselves and others, how can they possibly expect to succeed?

Look Potential in the Eye

On the other hand, people with a high level of verbal self-awareness will look inward or glance away just long enough to access high-producing thoughts. They then put their focus forward. When FM Sellers look another person in the eye, they become acutely aware that the words they use to describe any situation really do matter. This is why they check in to see where they look when they speak.

Experts in the field of Neuro Linguistic Programming (NLP) have also watched people as they communicate. Experiments in visual accessing actually map out where people focus their eyes as they retrieve specific information housed in the brain. When individuals construct images in their minds, recall events, remember sounds or smells, access feelings, or even talk to themselves, their eyes move to one of six different visual points. The points correspond to how they process their information.

Reconnect or Disconnect

From what I've noticed, after retrieving information, most people skip over the next step. They fail to reconnect with their buyer. For this reason it's important to ask yourself, "Am I aware of where I look after I access information and am about to speak?" Where you look determines if you're about to deliver a memorized sales presentation or if you are in the moment as you respond to the person in front of you. Our eyes don't lie.

Kelly's Keepers
Successful sellers pay attention to
where they look when they speak.

It's All Clear Now

If you're not sure where you place your attention, my soon-to-be famous **Now I See You—Now I Don't** exercise will increase your verbal self-awareness. Here are the instructions. Before you open your mouth, plant the thought in your mind that you'll look to see where your eyes focus when you speak. Then whenever your focus isn't on the listener, instruct your inner voice to say things like "You're not looking at the person" or "Be in the moment" or "Hello, are you even aware of what you're saying?"

Don't ask me why this exercise works. All I know is that when people set the intention to increase their verbal self-awareness, it happens. They're in the moment. Now they can master their ability to think conscious thoughts all the time.

Turn Off Your Mouth's Autoresponder

Once FM Sellers set the intention to be more verbally self-aware, several things are set in motion. Looking to see what you're focusing on causes you to stop and think before you speak—an action opposite of what most sales programs teach: "Remember class, as a good seller you must be able to think fast on your feet in all situations!"

Here's the problem with the think-fast-on-your-feet approach. If you haven't first trained yourself to think only powerful thoughts, then who knows what might come out of your mouth? Compelling research backs up this theory. In his book *Choices and Illusions,* Eldon Taylor says that "thirty years ago, Benjamin Libet showed that there is activity in the subconscious within milliseconds before a conscious thought occurs. In other words, our so-called conscious thoughts are given us by our subconscious."[1]

Great—our subconscious minds think for us. That's evidence enough to cause most people to stop and think before they talk.

Excuse Me While I Pause

A great way to stop your mouth before it leaps happens when you use another of my elaborate inventions, the **Intentional Pause**. As simple as the solution may seem, to be quiet can be one of the biggest challenges most people face. We live in a society addicted to noise and busyness. Even a nanosecond of silence has the potential to terrify the most experienced seller. However, in this situation, a moment of silence really can be golden.

Here's What I Meant to Think

Just as it sounds, the Intentional Pause requires you to pause and think before any self-defeating thoughts lodged in your unconscious mind can jump out. Here's a surprise: When you train yourself to turn off your mouth's autoresponder, your ability to think fast on your feet actually improves. Here's why: the precious seconds it takes to do the Intentional Pause put you in charge of what comes out of your mouth. Now the question becomes: When you stop long enough to hear what you think, do you like what you hear?

Turn On Your Powerful Communication

Even a subtle shift in the way you think can move your business forward. Unfortunately, when asked "What are your goals for this year?" far too many professionals talk about what doesn't work and back their viewpoints with endless negative evidence. Within seconds, AM Sellers separate themselves from FM Sellers.

Success-Limiting Language

Before they ever speak with clients, AM Sellers slam the brakes on their success when they fill their conversation with phrases like "Times are tough," "I will try to get new business," and "It's hard to get ahead today." Saying "It's hard to get ahead today" broadcasts a dream-killing message to themselves and others: "I don't believe I have what it takes to be successful." What buyers in their right minds would hand money over to these sellers?

Success-Enhancing Language

FM Sellers embed action thoughts into their subconscious minds. They voice, "I am ready, willing, and able" to describe their goals. What transforms this language into results is the clarity of FM Sellers' intentions.

"I am ready, willing, and able to get more clients" is a nice idea. However, what unleashes a very clear and confident intention is more specific: "I am ready, willing, and able to *double* the number of clients I have." FM Sellers have trained their minds to use language that builds success in any market and under any circumstance.

Kelly's Keepers
Negative thoughts = negative outcomes
Positive thoughts = positive outcomes
What have you thought about lately?

Say It Like You Mean It

If you don't like what comes out of your mouth, rewind your audio and hit delete. Replace any **Success-Limiting Language** with **Success-Empowering Language.** As I have discovered on more than one occasion, we are the ones who set the stage for our own triumph.

To aid in your growth, examples of Success-Empowering Language are listed in the following chart. There's also a place for you to write down your top two Success-Limiting comments. In the next column you can record more powerful Success-Empowering statements.

PERSONAL VOCABULARY REFRAME

Success-Limiting Language	Success-Empowering Language
1. "Times are tough."	"There is more than enough business for everyone!"
2. "I will *try* to get new business."	"I *will* get new business!"
3. "It's hard to get ahead today."	(FYI, here's my response to "It's hard to get ahead today": It is if you say so.)
	Don't reframe—just delete this thought from your brain!
4. _____	_____
5. _____	_____

What You Think Is What You Become

East Indian visionary, activist, and change maker Mahatma Gandhi summed up the thoughts-produce-outcomes theory best when he said, "A man is but the product of his thoughts. What he thinks is what he becomes."

Turn Up the Volume of Your Income

Almost everyone I've ever met has, at one time or another, recited a doom-and-gloom anecdote about money. This included me.

It was a quiet Tuesday afternoon, a few years into my speaking career, when I found myself sitting at my desk gazing forlornly at my bank statement. Suddenly the voice in my head wailed, "I'm so broke." A shudder of fear went down my back.

Forgetting that business was cyclical and most companies took vacations and didn't book speakers or consultants in August, I whined, "I'll never work again. The phone hasn't rung in two days . . . or has it been two weeks?" Then an even louder voice screamed, "This is the story you're telling yourself? How do you expect to get ahead with this attitude?"

Tell Me It Wasn't True

Yes, it appeared that yet another negative belief pattern had a hold on me. In addition to my sales-sabotaging thoughts, I had an extensive list of money-sabotaging thoughts. However, I wasn't alone. Many messages about money are passed on from family, society, and even the media. These messages are so entrenched in the subconscious mind that they threaten to bankrupt even the most well-intentioned person.

Some of the most common money statements professionals have churned out include: "You have to work hard for the money," "Money doesn't grow on trees," and the ever-popular "You get what you deserve." All of these sound very self-sabotaging.

Do Negative Money Thoughts Cost You?

Yes, our thoughts and beliefs about how easy or hard it can be to make money really do influence our ability to succeed. This includes influencing the ability to sell—especially the ability to sell high-end products and services. Over the years I've noticed that harboring negative thoughts about money ends up costing sellers precious business.

If you've ever thought to yourself, "I know they'll think the price is too high" or "I should give a discount," it's a safe bet that you've got a negative thought pattern around money. People project their thoughts of lack and limitation into each sales situation. That's why it's so important to get a handle on your money thoughts before you sell anything.

Kelly's Keepers

Thoughts about how easy or hard it is to make money influence your ability to sell—especially your ability to sell high-end products and services.

Think BIG—It Pays Off

Real estate tycoon and big money maker Donald Trump was on to something when he said, "As long as you are going to be thinking anyway, you might as well think *big*!"

If your income is in need of an overhaul, then do an internal audit. Tune in and listen to hear what you really think about money. If you don't like what you tell yourself, reframe your thoughts immediately.

Kelly's Keepers

Raise your thoughts about money to raise your income.

On the following page is a common negative money thought reframed into a powerful money-manifesting belief. Examples of other negative thoughts about money are listed too, along with a place to record your personal negative money messages. You can then reframe the costly money statements into powerful money-making beliefs.

SUCCESS-LIMITING MONEY MESSAGE EXERCISE

Success-Limiting Money Messages	Success-Enhancing Money Messages
1. "Money doesn't grow on trees!"	"Money does grow on trees. It's paper!"
2. "You have to work hard for money."	
3. "You get what you deserve."	
4. "I am so broke."	
5.	
6.	

If you were stumped about how to reframe any of those examples, here are my answers. "You have to work hard for money" becomes "Money comes easily." "You get what you deserve" turns into "There is more than enough for everyone." "I am so broke" is replaced with a thought that also popped into my head on that mind-numbingly quiet Tuesday afternoon: "I am just clearing space in my bank account for all the new money that's coming my way." For the record, for the next few years, I cleared more than enough space in my bank account for all the new money that was to come my way!

Kelly's Keepers
Rich thoughts make nice bank deposits.

As we've just explored, the story you tell yourself about how hard or easy it is to make money becomes the reality which deposits itself into your bank account. You'll now discover how all the powerful thoughts, when put together, can really pay off. The time is right to talk about how your thoughts can increase your audience of loyal customers.

Increase Your Audience of Loyal Customers

Oprah Winfrey has one of the most recognizable names and brands in the world. She also has one of the most loyal audiences of viewers ever known to humankind. This didn't just happen by accident; it happened by design. Oprah has made it her mission to live her best life and to help others do the same. Those thoughts touch something in her viewers. People who don't connect with her message can simply turn the channel and tune into another person's message.

What You Think Is Who You Get

As the Oprah example demonstrates, what people think *attracts* certain people to them. The same principle applies to the type of customer who's drawn to you. If someone connects with how you think, then that person will spend time with you and most likely buy from you.

If they don't connect with your way of thinking, they'll soon look for a seller whose style is a better fit. Think about yourself as a customer. Don't you prefer to work with a seller who understands how you tick? When asked, most people say yes without hesitating.

In essence, the way you think either attracts a buyer to you or it doesn't. It's a powerful reality. Yet few people know how to prosper from this awesome life principle. Once you discover how to use your thoughts to be a magnet and attract a loyal audience of buyers, there's no turning back.

The best way to predict the future is to create it.

PRESIDENT ABRAHAM LINCOLN;
REINTRODUCED BY PETER F. DRUCKER, MANAGEMENT VISIONARY

What Vibe Do You Give Off?

Ask yourself, "What do I really think about when I speak to a potential client?" Take your time exploring the question. Your answer could change everything. You see, when people interact on the phone or in person, an *energetic connection* is made. That connection can ignite the relationship or make it fizzle. Let me explain how this works.

Research shows that everything contains *molecular energy*. That includes our thoughts. They too contain energy. Yes, you read that correctly. Thoughts have energy—even Oprah's thoughts. When you have a thought about something, it produces an emotion. The emotion charges the energy in the thought. That charge or vibration will attract people of similar energy to you.

Positive or Negative—It's All Energy

To break it down even further, we will compare two types of thoughts—positive and negative—and the energetic charge that they produce. When you think positive thoughts, you feel good. Those good feelings raise your energy. Raised energy shows up as a high energetic frequency or vibration in your body. "Wow, does she ever give off great energy [a great vibe]!"

When you think negative thoughts, you feel down. Feeling down lowers your energy. This shows up as a low energetic frequency or vibration in your body. "Wow, he really is a downer [gives off a bad vibe]!"

Like a magnet, similar energy attracts similar energy. This same principle determines the type of customer drawn to you. What a person thinks and the emotional energy transmitted from those thoughts attract people with similar energy.

Your Thoughts Magnetize People

If you and your client think similar thoughts, you will find each other in a crowded room faster than you can shout, "Show me the money!" The energy produced from your combined thoughts turns you both into walking magnets. In essence, your thoughts and the energy attached to the emotion of your words determine what and whom you'll connect with.

When my thoughts focused on lack, scarcity, and fear, life was hard. The clients I attracted tended to be needy deal-seekers. As soon as my thinking shifted to thoughts of abundance and success, life got easier. I felt great. Even better, the feel-good clients who found me were professionals who were ready, willing, and able to invest in their own success. Not only that, but they were also excited to work with me.

Hallelujah! My stint in thought rehab had paid off. My new high-frequency thinking tapped me into the positive effects of manifesting. People and situations that were the perfect fit for the new and improved me were showing up—daily!

Put Your Thought Energy to the Test

You can test the frequency of your own thoughts with my purely unscientific thought/energy experiment. It demystifies how what you think becomes the opportunities, income, and clients you attract.

1. Read the following sentence and observe how you *feel*. (For the experiment, it's important to put the emphasis on the word *want*.)

Say to yourself: "I *want* great clients."

Ask yourself: How do I feel right now?

2. Read the following sentence and observe how you *feel*. (For the experiment, it's important to put the emphasis on the word *ready*.)

Say to yourself: "I am *ready* for great clients."

Ask yourself: How do I feel right now?

3. Here's the final check-in.

Ask yourself: "Which statement raised my energy, and which one lowered it?"

When participants do this exercise in OutSell Yourself seminars, you can actually feel the energy in the room as it lowers and rises. The low frequency produced from the word *want* seems to drain the lifeblood out of people. The high frequency emitted from the word *ready* shakes people up—in a good way!

About now you might be thinking, "Right. It's one thing to know how to think positive thoughts. But to do it all the time— that's a whole other story." If that's the case, then let me say you're absolutely right. To be able to think positive thoughts on a consistent basis is a whole other story. So let's cut to the chase. Read this next section. Do what it says, and the whole other story will have a happy ending.

Stay Tuned for Good News

Once clued into the benefits of thinking high-frequency thoughts, I promised myself to think only positive thoughts and to give thanks for all the good that came my way. I was on a mission! My new goal was to consistently send out high-energy messages to keep manifesting those great outcomes.

I'd already experienced positive results as I attracted new clients. Then when I thought positive thoughts about money, the contracts got even bigger. There seemed to be no end to what could be manifested. That was evidence enough for me. When it came to producing great outcomes, not only was I able to think it, feel it, and see it, but I was also ready, willing, and hopefully able to keep my success on a roll. However, in the beginning of this process, there were some days when my promise was easier to keep than on other days.

> *Nurture your mind with great thoughts,*
> *for you will never go any higher than you think.*
> BENJAMIN DISRAELI, BRITISH PRIME MINISTER

I Feel Good—I Think

To stay on course, I came up with a very simple emotional check-in method. All I had to do was to stop and observe my feelings. Did I feel *good* or *bad*? Was my energy *low* or *high*? If I felt bad, then I'd switch to a high-frequency feel-good thought.

For example, when a statement such as "I don't know if I'll get the contract" popped out of my mouth, my stomach would tighten and my energy would drop. The low-frequency thought left me with a bad feeling. Unfortunately, it would find its energetic match. In this case it would be an equally bad outcome—not getting the contract. Like attracts like.

To turn things around quickly, I would create a mental picture of the opposite outcome: the vision of me getting the job. Then I'd imagine how good it would feel to sign the contract, hold a big fat check in my hand, and be excited to work with the client. (I don't know about you, but I'm salivating as I write this. Okay, back to the story.) The new positive vision would set in motion a high-frequency charge of energy—as in charge forward! Now I liked what I was about to attract!

Know that what you seek also seeks you.
AUTHOR UNKNOWN

The Happy Ending

As promised, this story does have a happy ending. Consistent high-performance FM Sellers leave nothing to chance when it comes to selling. This is exactly why they train themselves to think positive thoughts—thoughts that make them feel good and send out a high-frequency vibration ready to attract its energetic match.

If you don't like what you're thinking and it leaves you with a bad feeling, change the station. Instead, tune in to a positive thought so that you feel good. Then fasten your seat belt. You just let loose a good high-frequency vibration, and only good will come from it.

Thoughts are real and what we think really does matter.
FRED ALAN WOLF, PH.D., QUANTUM PHYSICIST

Positive Thinkers Take Action!

Natalie Pace, number one Wall Street stock picker and author of *Put Your Money Where Your Heart Is*, and I recently explored how people's thoughts influence everything from their quality of life to their prosperity. Natalie summed the whole thing up this way:

The most important word in the "Law of Attraction" is action. Your thoughts point you in the right direction, but you must then ACT according to that which you desire in order to achieve results. And you must act consistently and diligently—even habitually. The bigger the dream, the longer it takes to get there and the more magnificent the results! Think of the Golden Gate Bridge, Machu Picchu, the Colosseum, and even the Apollo spaceship. These were all built by positive thinking act-ors!

It Worked for Me

Natalie's views certainly resonated with me. Once I grasped how dynamic the relationship was between my thoughts and the outcomes produced, everything in my life changed, including my actions. The next step to seal the deal on my long-term success was to truly understand why my products and services were worth the money I was ready to receive. Only then was I able to figure out the best way to present myself and my solutions to my ideal client.

Moving Forward

You now have the essential tools to train yourself to think high-frequency thoughts. Using these new skills makes it possible to dial into the FM Seller's fabulous success-manifesting station. Now we will take things up a notch. You are about to **Unleash Your Real Value.**

OPEN YOUR MIND TO SUCCESS—RECAP

Here's a quick recap of the main points we discussed to Open Your Mind to Success:

Success or Failure—It's All in Your Mind

It is not luck which determines a seller's success. What you think has the biggest influence on your success. Self-defeating thoughts can quickly become self-fulfilling prophecies. You may need to fire yourself and start over.

Tune To the FM Seller's Success Station

FM Sellers (Focused Manifesters) tune into high-frequency thoughts. AM Sellers (Aimless Manifesters) replay their life-is-tough-and-then-you-die standards daily.

Tune Out Static Interference

Tune out the static interference which negative self-talk can create—unless you want to stay stuck in old patterns.

Tune In Your Verbal Self-Awareness

Tune in a high level of verbal self-awareness. Your thoughts are real, and the words you use to describe any situation really do matter.

Turn Off Your Mouth's Autoresponder

Turn off your mouth's verbal autoresponder. There is activity in the subconscious milliseconds before a conscious thought occurs. So stop and pause before your mouth leaps into action.

Turn On Your Powerful Communication

Turn on your most powerful communication with Success-Empowering Language. It enables you to speak thoughts which fuel your success.

Turn Up the Volume of Your Income

You turn up the volume of your income with positive money messages. Thoughts about how easy or hard it can be to make money will influence your ability to sell—especially your ability to sell high-end products and services.

Increase Your Audience of Loyal Customers

Like a magnet, the vibration of your thoughts and the attached high-frequency emotions will inevitably find their magnetic match. This makes it possible for you and your perfect customers to find each other with ease.

Stay Tuned for Good News

Good News! When you take charge of what comes out of your mouth, you manifest positive outcomes.

3

Unleash Your Real Value

You think some of the most powerful thoughts known to humankind. Excellent! Your products and services are top-notch. Awesome! Your business card would make billionaire Bill Gates take notice. Way to go! You're in a fantastic position to sell . . . unless you haven't sold yourself on how valuable your products and services are. In that case, in spite of how great the package appears, the chances of selling your ideal clients on why they should invest tons of cash are bleak.

Far too many people haven't defined why their offerings are worth the big bucks—or any bucks, for that matter. Regrettably, they work too hard for the money. Even when you think thoughts like "I'm going to make lots of money," if you end up undervaluing your worth, it shows up as an income lower than it needs to be, even with a decent close ratio. I know. I've been there, done that, and have the t-shirt to prove it. It just doesn't pay to sell yourself short.

Don't Sell Yourself Short—It Doesn't Pay

If you don't buy why your products and services are worth the money, you'll never get a chance to unleash your real value. Even worse, guess what ends up being presented to your potential buyer? Brace yourself for this answer. It isn't flattering.

Your customer will come face-to-face with a person whose body language lacks confidence and who has a hesitant tone of voice. Worse yet, weak-kneed sellers often make deals that would make a dollar store seem expensive. This demonstrates the principle that thoughts are real and what you think ultimately attracts what you get. Let's face it. If deep down you don't truly believe in your worth, why would the customer?

Kelly's Keepers

When you recognize the real value of your goods and services, you avoid deep discounting.

The Signs of Undervaluing Are Everywhere

Many sellers are in denial about how much they undervalue their worth. They come up with endless excuses to justify why they can't charge full fee. I spent years in heated negotiations with myself over my fees. Some of the reasons for needing to slash prices and the best of the worst justifications I've heard from others are listed here for you.

SURE SIGNS YOU'RE NOT SOLD ON THE VALUE OF YOUR PRODUCTS AND/OR SERVICES

You tell yourself any or all of the following:

- My field/industry is very competitive, so my prices have to be low.

- My overhead is minimal. I can pass the savings on.

- Everybody wants a deal, so I give one before they ask. Smart of me, isn't it?

- Times are tough. You can't charge what you used to.

- I'm just starting out. When I get more experience, I'll charge more.

- If I don't discount my prices, they'll buy from someone else.

- I need to make my sales quota.

- Wow, that was easy. I knew I should have charged more!

If any of the statements hit home, beware. You could quickly scare off your ideal client. Instead, the notorious bargain-hunter could become your next buyer. They love sellers who undervalue their own worth and the worth of their products and services. Granted, you could argue, "Well, at least I made a sale," as I used to tell myself . . . until I finally woke up and owned up to what it had really cost me to get those sales.

Not Every Sale's Worth the Money

The financially stringent customer tends to be very high maintenance. This customer often wants all the frills and lots of attention for rock-bottom prices. After you work your butt off for pennies, their referral sounds like "I really recommend ABC Company. They're good and they're cheap." What a horrifying referral. What a horrifying sales trap. You're not only selling yourself short, but you're also wasting time with the wrong customer.

Avoid Being All Things to All Buyers

When asked "Who's your ideal client?" the typical answer most sellers shout with conviction is "anyone who will buy!" Unfortunately, that's not how things work. You are not selling to the whole world, as many sellers hope. As demonstrated in chapter 2, "Open Your Mind to Success," the energy of your combined thoughts triggers the connection. However, as our bargain-hunter customer illustrated, it's the value that you place on yourself, your products, and your services which determines who sticks around to buy—at full price.

Here's the best-case scenario: If you're selling high-end products or services, with lots of extras, your ideal customer will be the one who'll gladly pay for that value. If you're selling lower-priced commodities, which means low to no frills, your ideal buyer will be the one looking for lower-priced stuff.

The confusion comes when sellers lack a clear vision of the worth of themselves and their product and services. They end up discounting to get the sale or try to be all things to all buyers. You only unleash your real value when you are clear about what you offer and who it is for.

I don't know the key to success,
but the key to failure is trying to please everybody.
BILL COSBY

Sell Yourself First to Make Money

Once you identify the true value of your *expertise*, *goods*, and *services*—regardless of whether your offerings are high- or low-end—you can actually increase your income. And there's a good reason why: People who are sold on their worth simply won't give things away. They also won't waste time trying to sell to the wrong buyer. There are no ifs, ands, or buts about it. A very smart guy taught me that.

Don't Waste Time with Window Shoppers

Some students are teachers in disguise. Matthew, a participant in the first self-employment education program I ever taught for, was a marvel to me. Matt excelled in business. He recognized his value and the value of what he offered. He also believed, with certainty, that his ability to think it, feel it, and see it would move him forward. As a result, he would take the time to think through his plan for selling.

Another of the secrets to Matthew's success was that early in his career, he put a face and a name to his perfect buyer. In essence, Matthew identified his niche market. He could easily describe his ideal buyers and what they expected from him and his products and service. He knew exactly how much they were willing to pay. He even knew how and where to market so that his ideal customers would find him!

Every action Matt took, from packaging to marketing and selling, was focused on meeting the needs of his ideal buyer. This gave him the backbone to charge what his products were really worth. During our time together, I never once saw Matthew waste time with the window shoppers or bargain hunters. Matthew was a true FM Seller, in direct contrast to others who undervalued their worth, misidentified their buyers, and told stories a mile long to rationalize why the "jerk" didn't buy from them.

Whenever you see a successful business,
someone once made a courageous decision.
PETER F. DRUCKER

Niche Market to Make Money

It can take courage to charge top dollar and unleash your real value. Matthew was able to tap into that courage, and a whole lot more, by using a super-duper strategy to define his niche market.

If you like technical-sounding strategies, I wrote a great one for you: Define the real value of your products and services by assessing their worth in relation to the expectations of your niche market and the marketplace. (Are you still awake?)

Here's a non-techie formula: Ask yourself if your product or service provides a temporary, short-term, or long-term solution. Next, find out the level of customer service and expertise the end-user would expect from you and your solution. Finally, set your price to match what someone *should* pay for all of that value. And voilà, you've identified your perfect customer! (Do this and unleash your real value.)

Learn from Matthew's Success

Once Matthew made the connection that customers segment themselves into specific niche markets based on what they want from a product/service and seller, everything came together for him. He soon recognized the tremendous value of looking at the sale from his clients' point of view. Matthew determined, with certainty, that his buyers were prepared to pay top dollar. He also realized that it was his job to step up and deliver that value. This he did—time and time again.

The same method I taught to Matthew and hundreds of other professionals to define their niche market and unleash their real value is here for you too.

Choose a Price: Low, Medium, or High

The marketplace in almost any industry commonly has three price ranges for products and services: *low, medium,* and *high.* As Matthew found out, customers are attracted to specific price ranges and have very distinct expectations for each.

To demonstrate how price ranges work, we'll use retail stores as an example. Retail stores selling similar products could look like this: A dollar store fits into the low price range, a midsize independent store fits into the medium price range, and a large corporate chain store fits into the high price range.

LOW, MEDIUM, AND HIGH NICHE MARKETS

Typical Price Range	Retail Snapshot
Low	Dollar store
Medium	Midsize independent or franchise store
High	Large corporate chain

At each location, the price point and the quality of the product vary; so does the level of expertise and help provided by the person serving you. In addition, the types of warranties and/or aftercare you would or wouldn't receive differ. In essence, you get what you pay for. This pricing and expectation concept applies to your products and services too.

Define What You Offer—Your Market Will Follow

When you define what you offer, your market will follow. The **Package, Price & Target Market Exercise** found on the following pages walks you through how to do just that. The exercise has my personal Simple-Easy-Doable stamp all over it. Within minutes, you will know how to describe the features of what you provide, establish your price, put a face to your ideal customer, and target your marketing efforts. This will put you in the best position to charge what you're worth.

Kelly's Keepers

When you believe in the value of your products and/or services, so will others.

My Prices Are Already Set

If your prices are already set by your supplier [company, franchiser, supplier, industry . . .] and you are asking yourself, "Would I get anything out of doing the Package, Price & Target Market Exercise?" the answer is yes.

Lots of sales reps, agents, and others who sell prepriced merchandise and services waste their time selling to the wrong person. Sellers of medium-to high-end goods and services most often misidentify buyers. Whenever I hear a statement such as "I have to compete with the prices of the Big Box stores or I'll lose the sale," alarm bells go off. (A Big Box store typically has a limited selection of products with minimal features and benefits.)

The problem is not the price. Once again, it's that the wrong customers are being served. These buyers aren't comparing an apple to an apple. They are trying to compare a fresh apple to canned applesauce. So why discount the price of a premium apple to make it fit an applesauce budget? It makes more sense to send these buyers on their way. You will get better results if you put your time and effort into targeting the right customers. Then you can sell them a bushel or two of premium apples at full price.

Let's Unleash Your Real Value

Finally! It's time to unleash your real value. The Package, Price &
Target Market Exercise is divided into two sections: Selling Your
Services and Selling Your Products. Go to the section that applies
to what you sell. If you offer both services and products, check out
both sections. Within each are the tools to define what you offer,
your specific price range, and your ideal niche market buyers.

Kelly's Keepers
Experts THRIVE—Generalists Barely Survive.

Write a Marketing Plan Too

As you do the Package, Price & Target Market Exercise, write
down key places and ways to promote to your market. It is easy
to do. Once you identify who is in your ideal niche market, link
your promotion plans to your buyers' habits.

As an example, list the social or professional groups your
clients might belong to. Then schedule dates to show up and net-
work. If your buyers read specific publications, decide on the best
times to advertise or write articles. While you are at it, research
the blogs and online social networking sites where your buyers might hang out. Make a note to join, post comments, share
information, and subscribe for updates. These actions can get
your name in front of your niche market.

There are more opportunities than ever to connect with buyers. However, keep in mind that for any marketing effort to pay
off, your actions must be *specific* and *relevant* to your audience.
The only way to be targeted with your marketing is to have a very
clear picture of your ideal buyer. So sharpen your pencil, grab an
apple, and get ready to unleash your real value.

Selling Your Services—Package, Price & Target Market Exercise

Based on the you-get-what-you-pay-for theory, let's consider a fictitious basic example of how three different people who cut grass for a living would determine their fees, their niche market, and their promotion plan. In preparation for this exercise, extensive research was conducted on the lawn care industry. Granted, the information was pulled together while I was a teenager, which you'll read more about in a few minutes. However for now, please rest assured that it has stood the test of time. Ramon, a top-notch gardener that I know, gave it two thumbs up.

Similar considerations would apply to your business, all of which will help you to establish how valuable your services are and the market that will gladly pay for what you offer.

Turn to pages 50 and 51 to see the "Establish Your Service Package, Price & Target Market" exercise.

Example
ESTABLISH YOUR SERVICE PACKAGE, PRICE & TARGET MARKET:

Price Range	Related Education, Expertise	Length of Experience	Range of Services	
Person #1 Low: $30 per job Generalist (Immediate Solution)	Cut mom's lawn	1 year	Cut lawn	
Person #2 Medium: $40 per job Specialist (Short-term Solution)	Worked for landscaper	3 summers	· Cut lawn · Edge flower beds	
Person #3 High: $65 per job Expert (Long-term Solution)	Degree in landscaping	4 years	· Cut lawn · Maintain flower beds · Recommend plants	

GRASS-CUTTING SERVICES

Equipment	Client Profile	Promotion Plan
· Bike to customer's home · Use customer's gas & lawn mower	· 70% Renters · 30% Owners · Houses less than $180K	· Classified ads in Penny Saver newspaper
· Truck with removable signs · Use own gas & lawn mower	· Homeowners · Houses $180K to $220K	· Mail flyers · Hand out home-made business cards
· Truck with logo · Use own gas & lawn mower with mulcher, trimmer, and more	· Homeowners · Houses $220K to $450K	· Network at home-owner association meetings · Get referrals from garden center · Hand out profes-sional business cards · Have a business phone number

As the chart shows, the lawn-care professionals priced their services based on how much relevant experience they had, the extent of their services, and the type of equipment used to get the job done. They then put together a promotion plan to match the lifestyle, habits, and income of their specific niche markets. Finally, they advertised to the market which seeks their specific services and price range.

A Price Range within a Price Category

Not to make this too complex, but there's another important thing you need to know: Each price category also includes its own low, medium, and high prices. For example, in the low price range for lawn care, there might be three service providers offering similar but not identical services. As a result, their prices ranged from $18 to $25 to $30, all within the lowest-priced niche market.

Lawn-cutting gal Kelly set her price at $18 because she simply cut the grass and then hopped on her bike and peddled off. (Yes, I really did have a lawn-cutting business in high school.) The competition, Mr. Manual Labor, charged $25 and could get away with it because he also bagged the grass clippings. This raised his value up a notch from Kelly's $18 service.

However, the real king of the low-priced lawn-cutting industry was Rich Richey. Good old King Richey charged $30 to cut the grass, bag the clippings, and then carry the bags to the curb—all of which he did before he hopped onto his bike to ride off to the next job, of course stopping just long enough to collect his cash.

Whew!

Who knew that cutting grass could be such a complicated business? Who knew that even for a low-priced service there could be three different price ranges that would appeal to three very distinct groups of niche market customers?

Charge Top Dollar for Your Services

As the highly competitive grass-cutting businesses pointed out, there are many factors to think about when identifying the right niche market for your service, all of which also determine the price range you can charge within that niche market—low, medium, or high.

Here are some things to consider, which you'll then be able to record in the chart below:

- Do you provide a generic, one-size-fits-all solution?
- Are your education and experience extensive enough for you to ask in-depth questions to determine your customer's needs and recommend several solutions?
- Do your clients look to you as an expert who educates them?
- Are you a member of the professional association in your industry?
- Have you received any media attention, awards, or industry distinctions?
- Are there licenses or industry competencies that would separate you from others in your field?
- Are you expected to take annual continuing education courses or training?
- How about relevant life experience? It is priceless too.

There is also value in the extras:

- Do you have a 1-800 number?
- Are you a specialist, such as a personal trainer who brings your own equipment to a client's home or office?
- If you're in a business like catering, do you advertise time-saving extras like table and dish rentals?
- Are you a coach, consultant, professional speaker, or other service provider who sends out e-newsletters or writes a blog or articles?
- Do you offer guarantees or after-sales support, training, or follow-up? If so, how extensive would they be?

All these extras combine to increase your value.

To determine your niche market, you also need to put together a profile of your ideal client. If you sell to individuals, the questions to mull over can include:

- Are they male, female, single, married, same-sex partners, divorced, or widowed?
- What is their average age?
- What do they do for a living? Are they students, work-at-home parents, retired?
- Where do they live?
- Do they own or rent?
- What are the typical education level, income, ethnicity, and lifestyle?

If you sell to businesses or professional associations, they too have a demographic profile. You need to consider:

- What is the industry?
- How old is the organization?

- How many employees, members, branches, etc., are there?
- What is the culture [mission, philosophy, goal] of the company or organization?

Okay, that was a long list. However, let's be honest, could it be dawning on you that you've been undervaluing your worth? If you answered yes, or even hesitated to think about it, fill in the chart found on the following pages.

ESTABLISH YOUR SERVICE PACKAGE, PRICE & TARGET MARKET

Industry Fee Range*	Related Education, Licenses & Training	Years of Experience	Affiliations & Accomplishments	
Low: $_____ Generalist (Immediate Solution)				
Medium: $_____ Specialist (Short-term Solution)				
High: $_____ Expert (Long-term Solution)				

*If you're not sure what others charge for similar services, read the section on "Discover What the Competition Charges" later in this chapter.

Range of Services & Extras	Client Profile	Promotion Plan

Selling Your Products—Package, Price & Target Market Exercise

Based on the you-get-what-you-pay-for theory, let's consider a fictitious basic example of how three different professionals who sell window coverings would determine what prices to charge, their niche market, and their promotion plan.

Similar considerations would apply to your business, all of which will help you to establish how valuable your products are and the market that will gladly pay for what you offer.

Turn to pages 60 and 61 to see the "Establish Your Product Package, Price & Target Market" exercise.

Example
ESTABLISH YOUR PRODUCT PACKAGE, PRICE & TARGET MARKET:

Price Range	Options, Features & Warranty	Before-Sale Service
Low: $18–29 Basic (Immediate Solution)	· Up to 3 style options · Standard width & length · Slats tilt in two directions (open or closed) · 2-year life expectancy	· Self serve (look at picture on box for details)
Medium: $30–49 Standard (Short-term Solution)	· 4 colors & material options · Covers windows up to 10 feet wide · Child & pet-safe cords · Limited lifetime guarantee · Minimal light blocking & UV protection for furniture	· We cut to size (Hope you measured it correctly!) · Trained to make product recommendations
High: $50+ Deluxe (Long-term Solution)	· 27 colors and 15 material options · Covers windows up to 40 feet wide · Child & pet-safe cords · Lifetime guarantee · Maximum light blocking & UV protection for furniture · Remote controlled blind raisers · Provides maximum privacy	· We electronically measure for you · Trained to make product recommendations · Offer style, material and color suggestions

SELLING WINDOW COVERINGS

After-Sale Service	Customer Profile	Promotion Plan
· Installation service NOT available · 1-800# if product is defective [or] · Take a number & line up at customer service (Don't forget to bring your receipt!)	· 60% Renters · 40% Owners · 80% Women · 30% Married · 25–60+ years · Income $25,000 to 45,000	· Weekly specials · Display ads in local papers
· Installation provided on weekdays	· 30% Renters · 70% Owners · 80% Women · 60% Married · 25–60+ years · Income $45,000 to 75,000	· In-store specials · Newspaper ads · Door flyers · Website
· Installation provided days, nights & weekends	· 25% Renters · 75% Owners · 80% Women · 60% Married · 30–60+ years · Income $75,000 to 125,000	· Mailers to existing clients · Phone campaign to past clients · Booth at home shows · Display ads in major magazines & newspapers · Blog · Website · E-newsletters

As the chart shows, each product was priced based on how extensive the options, features, and warranty were. Also taken into consideration were the amount and quality of service provided before, during, and after the sale. A promotion plan was then put together to match the profile and income of the specific niche market. Finally, the sellers advertised to the market which seeks their specific products and price range.

A Price Range within a Price Category

Not to make this too complex, but there's another important thing you need to know: Each price category also has low, medium, and high prices. (In case you skipped over this explanation in the "Selling Your Services" section, you can read about it now.)

For our example, we'll use the window coverings from the low price range. Let's say you go to a big no-frills chain store to purchase your window coverings. You've probably been to a store just like it—huge parking lot, warehouse-style bins, and sales staff wearing nametags pinned to company shirts.

Even though the selection of products might be minimal, you would still have a variety of window coverings to choose from. At first glance, the blinds might look similar but they actually have different features. It's the type of features that determines the range of prices.

In the low price range, the blinds range from $18 to $25 to $29. What a deal! For $18, you can buy a no-frills, standard-length blind. If it fits your window exactly, you lucked out. For $25, it comes in two different styles. For $29, things get even better. The blind comes in three different styles, with tighter slats that block out tons of sunlight. Well, that was easy to explain!

Now it's your turn.

Charge Top Dollar for Your Products

As the intricate world of window coverings just pointed out, there are many factors to consider when identifying the right niche market for your products, all of which determine the price range you can charge within that niche market: low, medium, or high.

Here are some things to consider, which you'll then be able to record in the chart below:

- What types of features do your products offer?
- What about your level of expertise? Do customers look to you as an expert who educates them on the options available?
- Are you skilled enough to ask pertinent product application questions and then recommend the best solutions to meet customers' needs and fulfill their wish list, or are you seen as merely an order taker?
- Do you take continuing education courses or ongoing training to stay current?
- Are there licenses or industry competencies that would separate you from other product sellers?
- Are you a member of the professional association in your industry?
- Have your products received any media attention, awards, or industry distinctions?
- Do you use the product(s) too? Your credibility is priceless!

There's also value in the extras:

- Does your company have a 1-800 number?
- Is consumer education, information, or product training available?

- Do you offer any guarantees, warranties, after-sales support, and/or follow-up? If so, how extensive would they be?

All these extras add up to increase the value of your product.

To determine your niche market, you also need to put together a profile of your ideal client. If you sell to individuals, the questions to mull over can include:

- Are they male, female, single, married, same-sex partners, divorced, or widowed?
- What is their average age?
- What do they do for a living? Are they students, work-at-home parents, or retired?
- Where do they live?
- Do they own or rent?
- What are the typical education level, income, ethnicity, and lifestyle?

If you sell to businesses or to professional associations, they too have a demographic profile. You need to consider:

- What is the industry?
- How old is the company or organization?
- How many employees, members, branches, etc., are there?
- What is the culture [mission, philosophy, goal] of the company or organization?

Okay, that was a long list. However, let's be honest, could it be dawning on you that you've been undervaluing the worth of your product(s)? If you answered yes, or even hesitated to think about it, fill in the chart found on pages 66 and 67.

ESTABLISH YOUR PRODUCT PACKAGE, PRICE & TARGET MARKET

Price Range*	Options, Features & Warranty	Licenses, Training & Education	Before-Sale Service
Low: $_____ Basic (Immediate Solution)			
Medium: $_____ Value-Added (Short-term Solution)			
High: $_____ Deluxe (Long-term Solution)			

*If you're not sure what others charge for similar products, read the section on "Discover What the Competition Charges" later in this chapter.

66

After-Sale Service	Customer Profile	Promotion Plan

Discover What the Competition Charges

If you set your own prices and aren't sure of the going rates, there are many ways to track them down. One quick method is online research. Internet search engines are set up to do keyword searches for websites, news stories, articles, blogs, and videos that pertain to specific topics. Start with the basics. Type in the name or a simple description of your product or service and see what shows up. The information you need could be a mouse click away.

Ask Aunt Mable—She's a Know-It-All

How about talking to family, friends, and others who may have purchased similar products and services? A word of caution: Don't say, "Hey, what did you pay for that?" People may think you are being pushy, as I found out the hard way. Sorry, Aunt Mable. Instead, it's better to soften the inquiry with "If you don't mind me asking, what does something like that cost?"

Associations and Industry Experts Tell All

You can also contact your professional association to find out going rates in your field or industry. Most associations track that information. Once armed with the data, use it as an opportunity to connect with more experienced experts in your field. They often have information and insights which could take you years to gather.

When speaking to the experts, ask, "How realistic are the numbers given by the association?" Sometimes the fees and prices are out of date or resemble a wish list. It's also vital to confirm, "What's *offered* for the money, and who would the *typical* client be?" Remember: To be able to compare an apple to an apple, you must first verify that it's not applesauce.

Your Direct Competition Bares All

Another great technique, in my humble opinion, is **Kelly's Just Ask Method**. I invented it to address a big need of mine. Over the years, as my skills, knowledge, and accomplishments increased, it was a natural transition to move from the generalist to the specialist and eventually to the expert market.

Each niche attracted specific clients with specific needs and expectations which I had to consider when setting my fees. The only challenge was that I didn't have a clue about what to charge each market. (It's funny how things can change. Today my accountant supplies me with endless evidence for why the fees need to be as they are.) However, back then, I called other experts who also offered keynote talks, seminars, sales programs, teleclasses, and coaching—my competition. It was a great way to collect the information and form strategic alliances.

If you take advantage of this technique, *please* don't use the tired opener, "Hi. I'm a student doing market research. Could I ask you a few questions?" No one believes it anyway. Keep it honest and stay in integrity. Use my script below.

"KELLY'S JUST ASK METHOD" FOR DETERMINING PRICES

"Hi, this is _____. I'm a sales and business expert [bricklayer, baker, candlestick maker.]

"I'm doing research to make sure that my rates are competitive and that I don't *undercut* anyone. [That grabs attention!]

"Those who participate in my survey will get access to the information I collect. You'll find out what the others charge and what they offer for the money. You'll also receive a profile of their typical market.

"However, I *will not* disclose the names of anyone who participates in the survey. You'll get only the survey results. Everyone's confidentiality is assured. Would you be interested in participating?"

Yes—Competitors Will Share Information

Are you wondering why your competition would agree to share coveted information? Well, it's quite simple. They need the information too. Self-employed folks tend to work in isolation, while people working for companies often feel as if they're operating in a vacuum. In this get-ahead, stay-ahead culture, it's enough work just to keep current in your area of expertise. Add to that the time it takes to sell and deliver your products and services. Suddenly, keeping all the balls in the air can be quite a juggling act.

Then *kaboom,* an opportunity to stay in the loop appears. Talk about a gift from the heavens. This could explain why the participation rate for surveys I've done has always been high. Other professionals who have used the script have also had great results.

> *The wisest mind has something yet to learn.*
> GEORGE SANTAYANA, PHILOSOPHER

Knowledge Increases Confidence

Once you find out the industry rates and what the customer gets for the money, you will never unknowingly undercharge. This assures that you get paid what your products and services are really worth. It will also raise your selling confidence.

Moving Forward

You unleashed your real value by identifying what makes you and your products and services so unique. The same process made it possible to package, price, and market to your ideal buyer. Now you are in a great position to appeal to your customer's real buying motivators . . . if you actually know what motivates a customer to sign on the dotted line. Even if you think you might know, do not take any chances. Turn the page and find out what it takes to stand out with buyers. We are about to **Tap Into Your Clients' Real Buying Motivators.**

UNLEASH YOUR REAL VALUE—RECAP

Here's a quick recap of the main points we discussed to Unleash Your Real Value:

Don't Sell Yourself Short—It Doesn't Pay

If you haven't sold yourself on the value of your expertise, products, and services, then the chances of selling others on investing tons of cash are pretty bleak.

Avoid Being All Things to All Buyers

Sellers who try to be all things to all buyers work harder than they need to, and they often get paid less than their products and services are really worth.

Niche Market to Make Money

Buyers are attracted to sellers and their goods and services when they meet very distinct needs. What is offered segments sellers into specific niche markets.

Choose a Price: Low, Medium, or High

Within each niche market, buyers expect to pay a certain price for all that is included with the goods and services. Typically the price categories are low, medium, or high, with additional price levels within each range.

Selling Your Services—Package, Price & Target Market Exercise

When you identify the appropriate price range for your services, you must consider variables such as your related education and/or expertise, length of experience, range of services, equipment, and a profile of your client.

Charge Top Dollar for Your Services

To charge top dollar in your niche market, you also need to clarify the extras that come with your services. All those extras add up.

Selling Your Products—Package, Price & Target Market Exercise

When you identify the appropriate price range for your products, you must consider variables such as the options, features, warranty, before-sale service, after-sale service, and a profile of your customer.

Charge Top Dollar for Your Products

To charge top dollar in your niche market, you need to also clarify the extras that come with your products. All those extras add up.

Discover What the Competition Charges

Do research to find out what the competition charges. This will ensure that you never unknowingly undercharge within your niche market. It will also raise your selling confidence.

Tap Into Your Client's Buying Movtivators

Wait! Before you even think about speaking to a client, you need to know the three important things that motivate someone to hire you or buy your products. This makes it possible to focus your sales approach with laser-beam accuracy.

It sounds simple enough. Yet almost 99 percent of the professionals who've attended my OutSell Yourself sessions can't say with certainty why someone purchased from them. Even veteran sellers can be hard pressed to come up with the right answer. Not knowing what really motivates a person to buy is sort of like playing darts with a blindfold on. You may or may not hit the mark every time . . . if you even get close to the board.

*If you don't know where you're going,
any road will take you there. That is, if you're lucky.*

AUTHOR UNKNOWN

3 Powerful Ps Motivate People to Buy

If you like quizzes and guessing games, I've got a great one for you. Just answer the Buying Motivator Quiz below. Good luck!

Three main things motivate a customer to select one seller's products and services over another. All three motivators start with the letter P. What are they?

BUYING MOTIVATOR QUIZ

What three things motivate and influence customers to purchase your products & services?

1. P _____

2. P _____

3. P _____

Time's up! The accounting firm Call When Things Don't Add Up, Inc. has tabulated the results. Drum roll, please, as we open the envelope. The three things that motivate customers to buy are: the person, followed by the product or service, and then the price—all of which we are about to talk about in more detail.

Put Your Best Foot Forward—It Pays Off

The person doing the selling is the number one thing that influences a customer to select one seller's service or product over another.

If you gasped "What? The price wasn't the number one buying motivator?" you are not alone. The first answer most sellers come up with is price. There's a good reason for this. Customers seem programmed to ask, "What's the price?"

Unfortunately, when you talk money with a client before building a buying relationship, you risk losing the sale. It's too soon in the conversation to talk about price. You and the customer haven't made a real connection. At this early stage, if they don't like the numbers, it's easy to say no. It's not personal. How could it be? The customer doesn't know you. So saying "Thanks, but no thanks" becomes a cut-and-dried decision.

Take the Focus off Your Price

If someone begins a conversation with "What's the price?" your best approach is to use a redirecting statement. This takes the attention off your price and puts the focus back on building trust, which is the key to forming a solid sales relationship. (Examples of redirecting statements are in chapter 5 under "Ask Kelly" in response to "What's the best thing to say to clients who begin the conversation with 'What's the price?'")

Right now it's essential to recognize that regardless of what a customer may have been conditioned to ask, what really tips the buying scales in favor of one product or service over another is the relationship between the buyer and seller.

Kelly's Keepers

A trusting relationship moves a buyer past
any concerns about "What's the price?"

Build Sales Relationships with Women and Men

Important news flash! With women, the world's largest buying market, it's crucial to build a sales relationship based on trust—before you attempt to sell them anything. Women don't just buy stuff. Women invest in goods and services . . . with sellers they trust.

Before she even considers whether that will be "cash, check, credit card, or debit," a woman needs assurance that you have her best interests at heart. Sellers who are out to make a quick sale had better look out. A woman will tune them out so fast their heads will spin. Then while a dazed vendor tries to figure out what just happened, she'll quickly move on to the professional who is ready to get to know her and what she is looking for.

Does this mean that men don't value a good buying relationship? Of course it doesn't. Men also seek out trusted sellers. They too want to buy from professionals who focus on meeting their needs. However, it's important to recognize that men typically decide on product and service solutions a lot faster than women.

When selling to a man, the getting-to-know-you trust-building phase is shorter than with a woman. Throughout the book, you will find a variety of trust-building questions which apply to both genders. You will also see the key differences in how you need to frame your questions to connect with women and to connect with men.

Keep in mind that before you talk products and services, both female and male buyers want you to understand what they're looking for. Neither will waste valuable time with the person who'll sell just about anything to boost their sales quota. Buyers want to deal with people they trust.

Kelly's Keepers
The number one buying motivator is a PERSON—YOU!

Be Real and Really Mean It

Because it is so vital to establish trust up front, I often provide a thought-provoking exercise in one of my OutSell Yourself sessions. I ask professionals a straightforward question: "If you were to overhear two of your clients talking about you, what positive thing(s) would they say?" The session participants then complete this sentence: "[Name] is a _____."

Some of the qualities people have declared for themselves include being a problem solver, advisor, excellent listener, dependable expert, guide, helper, proactive consultant, reliable solution provider, technical resource person, caring healer, facilitator of fun experiences, multitalented educator, and specialist in their field. The list of affirmative character traits seems to go on forever. The end result is powerful.

It is never too late to be who you might have been.
ATTRIBUTED TO GEORGE ELIOT & DINAH MARIA (MULOCK) CRAIK

When we see ourselves through a customer's eyes, things look different. It's as if a bar has been set to monitor our professional behavior. Suddenly we become very conscious of how our words and actions impact our ability to be authentic, trustworthy, and able to sell with integrity. To declare your intent to be real and really mean it, you can do a similar exercise. Simply take a minute to imagine how your customers would describe you and then finish the sentence below.

"In business, I am known as _____
_____."

Kelly's Keepers
Be real and really mean it.

Your goal to be the best you can be will pay off. Who you are and how you treat your customers are primary buying motivators. This leads us directly to the second most important buying motivator.

Let Your Products and Services Speak for Themselves

Second prize in the buying motivator contest goes to your products and services. This occurs for a good reason. When you take the time to develop a high level of trust by asking questions, buyers are more open to telling you about their needs. They're also more open to learning about your product and service solutions. You have earned your buyers' trust—your products and services will speak for themselves. You don't want to blow it now.

Kelly's Keepers
Your PRODUCTS & SERVICES are
the second important buying motivator.

Don't Blow It Now

So far so good. You asked questions, and your prospective customers have confidence in you, the person doing the selling—buying motivator number one. They are interested in hearing about your products and services—buying motivator number two. You are moving forward. However, you can quickly be back at square one if you try to fast-track the deal.

Do not, under any circumstances, launch into a tell-a-thon or brag-a-thon about your great stuff. No one wants to be sold. Besides, you risk boring people to death with your presentation. Even if you have the charisma of a rock star, it's estimated that most people's concentration drifts off every seven seconds. Plus, you can only hold a person's full attention for approximately 15 to 20 minutes. Instead, let them read your brochure if they have trouble getting to sleep some night.

You'll do best to continue to focus on the person in front of you. In customers' minds, your willingness to make an honest effort to understand them and their situation made a positive impression. They'll now pay closer attention as you discuss *potential* product and service solutions, which we'll cover in more detail in chapter 7, "Lead with Your Best Solution." This is the time to disclose the third and final buying motivator.

Kelly's Keepers
When clients trust sellers, they pay closer attention
to their products and services.

Price Too Expensive—That's Just an Illusion

Price is the third and final thing which motivates someone to buy from you. Yes, finally we got to the price. This is the same buying path you want your customers to follow. When you do a great job of building a relationship, then suggest products and services designed to meet real needs, customers place much less emphasis on price . . . even when you charge the highest rates in your niche market.

Kelly's Keepers
PRICE is the third buying motivator.

The Cheapest Price Doesn't Always Sell

When someone believes that you have the perfect solution, money can simply become a means to a great end. Think about your own buying habits. How many times have you justified spending more than you planned to be able to do business with someone you felt truly understood your needs? Who didn't oversell you? Who treated you with respect? Who you knew would follow up if you had any problems or questions after the sale? Even when you had set a firm budget, which you were determined to stick to?

If you're like almost every person I've ever polled, your answer would be, "Lots of times!" The justification is, "It may cost a bit more up front, but I know I'm getting exactly what I need, without a lot of hassle. And they'll look after me if there are any problems. This will save me money in the end." Yes, you sold yourself.

Kelly's Keepers
People will invest even more
when you offer the perfect solution.

Put It All Together

As we've seen, three important things motivate someone to buy. The process begins with a positive relationship between the buyer and you—the person doing the selling, followed by the customer's keen interest in your products and services, and finishes with the client's consideration of the price. Stunning revelations that only took me about a decade to link together!

Moving Forward

As we have seen, tapping into the three buying motivators made it easy to sell. What makes it even easier is knowing the right questions to ask . . . which we're about to discover in the next chapter, "**Sell without Selling.**"

TAP INTO YOUR CLIENT'S BUYING MOTIVATORS—RECAP

Here's a quick recap of the main points we discussed to Tap into Your Clients' Buying Motivators:

3 Powerful Ps Motivate People to Buy

Three powerful things motivate a customer to select one seller's products and services over another. It's the person selling, followed by the products and services offered, and then the price.

Put Your Best Foot Forward—It Pays Off

Trust builds between you and buyers when you take the time to understand them and their needs.

Build Sales Relationships with Women and Men

When selling to women, the getting-to-know-you trust-building phase is typically longer than when selling to men.

Be Real and Really Mean It

Seeing yourself through your clients' eyes helps you become conscious of the impact of your words and actions.

Let Your Products and Services Speak for Themselves

When you do a great job of building trust, buyers pay closer attention to your products and services.

Price Too Expensive—That's Just an Illusion

Once satisfied that you offer the best product and service solutions, customers will place less emphasis on the price.

5

Sell without Selling

"Kelly, how do you sell without selling?" That is the number one question I'm asked. My answer has always been the same: "You quit trying to sell. Instead you make it your goal to fully understand the customer before you talk about products or services."

As covered earlier, the number one buying motivator is the relationship between the seller and buyer. Your readiness to work with a client is what moves you to the top of the list of preferred vendors—not your ability to memorize and spit out a skillfully prepared sales presentation. This can be great news if you are comfortable in your own skin. It is horrible news for someone who unknowingly acts like the stereotypical salesperson who spends most of the time telling clients what they should buy.

I often wonder whether these sellers recognize how embarrassingly out of date they are. If they're not aware of how off-putting their behavior is, how will they change? I must confess that I was one of those people.

> *The reason for learning is not to know more*
> *but to behave differently.*
> SYDNEY BECKETT

Say Good-Bye to the Salesperson Act

My friends love to reminisce about some of my early struggles in business. "Remember when you started speaking professionally? You wore that tailored navy blue suit with the stiff white blouse. As soon as you put the clothes on, you acted like an anxious executive. That was so funny." Yeah, it was very funny. I'm still *not* laughing.

Something horrible happened when I stepped into my structured clothing. I acted like the world's slickest-sounding salesperson. My sales monologue sounded as if it were straight out of the play *Death of a Salesman*. The conversations were so formal they even scared me. Yes, Kelly the Business Wonder Woman had arrived to broker all contracts. Talk about creating drama.

I Wish I Were Joking

Back in the day, clients looked like dollar signs. How could they appear real when the person doing the selling had disconnected from herself? Not only did I look uncomfortable, but everything about my sales banter was unnatural. If I didn't know what a buyer needed, I faked my way through the conversation. I dreamed up endless solutions until my worn-out client finally whispered, "Yeah, that'll do." I was clearly out of my comfort zone. What was truly funny was that anyone hired me at all.

What Language Do You Speak?

I wasn't the only seller behaving this way. Many people have sounded like a salesperson at one time or another. What were we thinking? What customer in their right mind would tell that kind of seller what they really wanted or what the true budget was? Not me. I wouldn't trust anyone who tried to sound or even act like a professional seller. This means that I wouldn't even buy from myself. What an empowering thought.

Quit Selling—It Hurts My Ears

Today my sales conversations flow naturally. Nervous babbling has been replaced with an interactive Discovery Dialogue—to find out what the client really wants. By the time we've finished *talking*, so much has been revealed. It's obvious to us both what they're looking for and how I can help. But I didn't figure out how to do this overnight.

Have a Discovery Dialogue

To create comfort in my own selling skin, regardless of what I wore, I had to look at what I already knew. There must be a way to have fluid and natural-sounding sales conversations. I couldn't be a total loser . . . I hoped. After all, in my personal life I'd developed some terrific relationships.

The Psychology of Selling

Before opening the sporting goods business, I'd graduated with an honors diploma in Social Services. I had earned the highest marks in my class; surely I could figure out how to apply similar psychology and communication principles to selling. After all, regardless of the situation, don't we all desire to live our best life? People go for counseling because they want something to be improved. Aren't buyers after the same thing? Aren't they too looking for change? And I'm not referring to getting cash back from their dollar.

Consumers look to products and services to make life easier, to improve a situation, or to make them feel good. Companies also want results. They want to know if your solution will save them money, make them money, or improve brand recognition, systems, morale, customer service, or productivity. Yes, it was obvious: We turn to sellers for answers. However, before I could even consider suggesting buying solutions to my clients, I had to find the best way to uncover their real needs and expectations.

Cracking open textbooks from college . . . and cracking open my brain, I solved the first riddle: Develop a series of *interactive* and *nonthreatening questions* that would give insight into customers, the challenges they faced, and the best solutions for their situation. Excellent! The next step was to figure out how to put the questions into a logical order. Once again, I focused on what I already knew.

It's All about You!

When women meet socially, there's an unspoken agreement as to how the conversation will unfold. We tend to begin by asking *general* getting-to-know-you questions: "What do you do for a living?" "Do you have kids?"

As we feel more comfortable, we ask more *focused* questions: "How long have you been at your job?" "How old are your kids?" Then as the evening progresses, or in the time it takes to leave the women's washroom, we've built enough trust to ask *precise* questions: "How has business been in your industry?" "Are your kids addicted to YouTube?" "Do they spend hours on Facebook?" "How do you deal with it?"

There was my next answer: Blend the psychology of *why* each question is asked with the proven conversation pattern of women. This I did. Today, men and women in fields as diverse as coaching, wholesale product distribution, and retail sales use the same Discovery Dialogue techniques to sell without selling.

1-2-3 Discovery Dialogue

So that there's no margin for error, let's clarify the difference between a Discovery Dialogue and a sales presentation. A Discovery Dialogue is an interactive exchange between a seller and a customer. It is not a sales presentation. A sales presentation is a one-sided conversation that inhibits relationship-building, risks selling the wrong things, and turns people off! "We have 5,000 products, which I'll now explain in great detail. When I'm done talking, in about 45 minutes, you'll know exactly how these products will change your life . . . we hope. If not we have seventeen 1-800#'s that you can call . . . yada . . . yada . . . yada . . . blah . . . blah . . . blah...boring . . . boring . . . boring."

Ask Targeted Questions

When you have a Discovery Dialogue, *you* and the *customer* focus on finding out what's best for them. You do this by asking open-ended questions that begin with *who, what, when, where, how, if you,* and *tell me about.* All questions are targeted to draw out specific information. The customer's answers clarify everything from who are the end-users to what they need and expect to who is the real decision maker. Open-ended discovery questions do not require a yes or no answer. Those types of questions belong to persuasive selling tactics which are outdated and really annoy people,

   "If I were to show you a foolproof way to save money, would you buy today?!?"

   "NO! Get lost!"

Take the attitude of a student, never be too big to ask questions, never know too much to learn something new.

OG MANDINO, AUTHOR OF *THE GREATEST SALESMAN IN THE WORLD*

10 Great Reasons to Have a Discovery Dialogue

1. Eliminates unfocused and boring sales presentations
2. Gets the client talking and involved
3. Builds a trusting relationship
4. Gains a lot of information in a short amount of time
5. Focuses in on the real problems and opportunities
6. Gives busy clients and customers a chance to plan out loud
7. Helps the buyer to establish criteria for decision making
8. Assists the end-user to justify why your products/services are worth the money
9. Speeds up the decision-making process
10. Results in larger sales, repeat business, and better referrals. (Okay, this last point gave three reasons to have a Discovery Dialogue . . . but they're great reasons, don't you think?)

If those ten or so reasons were compelling enough for you to want to use the Discovery Dialogue techniques, you'll love what comes next.

Kelly's Keepers

A Discovery Dialogue lets both buyer and seller know what's really needed.

Keep Your Conversations Flowing

During a Discovery Dialogue, the questions take you through three levels of information gathering: *general*, *focused*, and *precise*. This three-step pattern applies to all sales encounters. Depending on your customer and their situation, you fine-tune the phrasing and formality of your questions. For example, "Who else in your *company* will be using the product?" becomes "Who else in your *family* will be using the product?" In both circumstances, the question uncovers any additional product/service features and benefits that should be made known to the buyer later on. As a Discovery Dialogue case study, we will use the scenario of a business-to-business seller speaking with a potential client.

Get in the Ready Position

To prepare for the conversation, our B2B seller will preselect some general questions to ask. These are the questions that build a relationship between the buyer and seller and establish background information. There's nothing more embarrassing than writing up an order or contract and not knowing the name of the person you talked to, their role, or what their company does. You only have to make that mistake once, or five times, before you change your habits!

Our seller will also do some preresearch before speaking with the buyer. The goal is to get up to speed on the company, the industry, and any trends. Don't think that it's only multinational corporations and large retailers who must do their sales homework. The need to do preresearch in order to look like a pro who asks useful questions applies in all industries and fields. Consultants, entrepreneurs, sales agents/reps, and others also benefit from doing groundwork. Knowing your buyer is what separates the expert from the generalist. (Think back to chapter 3, "Unleash Your Real Value.") Experts thrive, while generalists barely survive.

It's Easy to Collect Information

For our B2B seller, collecting research prior to the sales meeting can be as simple as reading information from the company's website. To really stand out in the knowledge department, our expert will also do a few Internet searches to uncover industry facts and data, recent articles, reports, blog postings, and announcements. Throughout the Discovery Dialogue, the seller will then confirm and insert what they know into the discussion.

Similar research tools are at your fingertips too. Even if you sell in a retail environment or to a client who contacts you first, you can collect key facts about the buyer in advance of any sales conversation. Remember when you completed the "Package, Price & Target Market Exercise" in chapter 3? To write the profile of your niche market buyer, you identified such things as their habits, needs, and tastes. This information is invaluable and ready to use.

For example, let's say you sell high-end furniture in a retail store. Let's also assume that the majority of your buyers are couples ages 50 to 70. You would know ahead of time that most have downsized their homes. You could then introduce this fact into the conversation in the form of a general question: "Are you looking for full-sized furniture or smaller-scale pieces?" The inquiry reveals a lot, including the fact that you are expert enough to know to ask it. Now let's get back to our case study!

Kelly's Keepers
Preselling research separates experts from generalists.

Learn from a Used Car Salesman

Before our B2B seller begins the Discovery Dialogue, there is something important to know. People often share more information when they know *why* they're being asked the question. The unwritten Buyer-Beware Warning sparked that aha insight.

The warning states: "It's a customer's job to block a salesperson from overselling them." I think it came about in the late 1940s.

It was when the first pushy used car salesman caused a guarded customer to clam up or lose money. The Buyer-Beware Warning has been in existence ever since.

Therefore, instead of diving headfirst into the Discovery Dialogue, our seller will let the buyer know what's going on. As the car industry has taught us, it can be the kiss of death not to obtain a buyer's permission to ask questions—especially when selling to a woman.

Tell a Woman *Why* You're Asking

Women need to know *why* answering a seller's questions will assist them. Women won't buy into something, or won't buy much of anything for that matter, unless they know why it's in their best interests to do so. A female buyer needs to know why it will benefit her to disclose certain information. That's how women's brains are hardwired to react. (In chapter 7 under the heading "Give Women What They Really Want," you will find more detailed information to explain what causes this reaction.) For now, to play it safe, our B2B seller will get the buy-in to ask questions from all customers.

Kelly's Keepers
Women want to know why
answering your questions will assist them.

Put Your Agenda on the Table

Our seller will be honest and transparent when explaining why it's in anyone's best interests to share information. Here's an example of what our B2B seller will say: "Before we talk about products/services, I have a few quick questions to ask. Then I will fully understand your situation and will know the best solution(s) to recommend to you." In the buyer's mind, it now makes sense to answer the questions. They know why and how their answers will be used. Trust is forming.

> *If people like you they'll listen to you,*
> *but if they trust you they'll do business with you.*
> ZIG ZIGLAR, SALES EXPERT

When you phrase your own buy-in statement(s), be sure to sound like yourself. Otherwise you won't feel comfortable. Your customer will sense it too. Fortunately, our B2B seller feels composed enough to move the Discovery Dialogue forward. They are ready to ask some targeted questions.

General Questions

Our B2B seller will begin with general questions. Each inquiry assists in constructing a detailed client profile. Many of the general questions listed below serve a dual purpose. They can also be used as a preresearch checklist. As stated earlier, any facts, figures, and details collected ahead of time can be referred to throughout the conversation. The more information gathered in advance of the Discovery Dialogue, the better.

As you eavesdrop on the conversation, be sure to pay special attention to how our B2B seller incorporates some of their research findings into the Discovery Dialogue. Bear in mind that at this early stage, the objective is to understand the big picture.

About the Company
• Before we talk about products/services, I have a few quick questions to ask. Then I will fully understand your situation

and will know the best solution(s) to recommend to you. I understand that your company has been a leader in X for over twenty years. (The seller builds trust by stating the purpose of the questions. They also establish credibility by stating what their research revealed. They then use the Intentional Pause to encourage the buyer to share information—which often happens. People love to talk about themselves or, in this case, the company.)

- I understand that your company does X. What else does the company do [provide, offer]?
- How does your company [business, group, organization] operate?
- How many divisions [territories, franchises] are there?
- What is your specific role? (If you need to confirm the person's title, now's the time to do it.)

About the People
- What is the structure of your company [corporation, business, association]?
- How many employees [directors, members, franchises/franchisees] are there?

About the Situation
- How many people in your company [group, organization] will be using the product/service?
- Who are the people who will be using [benefiting from] the solution [product, service]?
- What are their [roles, titles, ages, gender (if appropriate)]?
- Whom do they report to?

Focused Questions

Our B2B seller is on a roll! They've asked a variety of questions and have a great understanding of the company and the players. Now they can delve a little deeper. By asking more focused questions, they will get a sense of why the client wants and/or needs what they are selling. Many sellers report, "At this point in the conversation, I feel as if I'm working in partnership with the client."

The getting-to-know-you general questions asked earlier demonstrated a sincere willingness to understand the customer and establish trust. It's now becoming a shared goal to find the best product/service solution(s).

Below are a variety of focused questions our seller might ask. Before posing any questions that require the customer to reveal sensitive or proprietary information, our B2B seller will state why it's of benefit to do so.

About the Situation

- So that I fully understand what's been happening, how would you describe your current situation [needs, wants, problems, challenges]?
- What isn't working with your present situation [supplier, product, service]?
- What do you think is contributing to this situation [problem]?
- How is this situation affecting you [your company, business, members, customers]?
- Tell me about your goals [visions, plans] for your company [department, team, organization].

About the Solution

- What would you like to be different [to be improved, to be corrected, for our product/service to do for you]?
- If you've used a similar service/product in the past, what worked well?
- What else would you need/want?
- Who else will need information about this?

Precise Questions

Excellent! Our seller has gathered important background information about the buyer and their company. They have also gained insight into the buyer's current situation and challenges. The time is ripe to ask precise questions. This provides the most in-depth picture of what the customer wants and doesn't want, as well as their expectations. It will also make it easier to figure out which customized solutions will work best. In addition, the seller can uncover any hidden decision makers and learn about the decision-making process—information that's worth its weight in gold! The following are precise questions our B2B seller could ask to wrap everything up.

About the Solution

- You mentioned that _____. Can you give me an example?
- What additional changes [results, solutions, outcomes] are you looking for?
- Who else would you like me to gather information from?
- What haven't I asked you that you'd like me to know?
- What price range are you looking to spend?

- How will you evaluate the effectiveness of the product/service?
- How does the decision-making process work?
- Will you be making a recommendation or giving the final go-ahead?
- Who else will be included in the decision-making process?
- What potential challenges or roadblocks might prevent your company from moving forward with this?
- What are our next steps?

The Top Seller's Award Goes To ...

Our B2B seller did a superb job! They asked top-notch questions and gathered valuable information in a very short period of time. Our seller learned about the company, the people, and their situation. They zeroed in on the type of results the customer is looking for, which will make it effortless to suggest targeted solutions. They are selling without selling. Now it's your turn.

Kelly's Keepers
Ask general, focused, and then very precise questions
to zero in on the real issues.

Change Your Questioning Style with Women and Men

Before you select the perfect questions to ask your customer, there is a crucial gender-based distinction you must know about. You can often ask more questions of a woman than of a man ... for a variety of reasons.

Focus on Uncovering the Problem—With a Woman

A woman will roll out the welcome mat to the seller who asks her a lot of useful questions. She also appreciates being asked to explain her circumstances or problem. A female buyer wants a seller to really get a handle on her situation and what she's looking for, before making made-to-order recommendations.

In a woman's eyes, if you have the ability to ask purposeful questions, listen to fully understand her needs, and offer customized solutions, you're a true expert. This is in direct contrast to how she feels about the seller who asks few questions and simply fires off generic solutions. Think about our used car salesman. Need I say anything more?

Focus on the Bottom Line—With a Man

Men turn to sellers to provide immediate expert solutions. Keep in mind a point made earlier: The goal for a man is to solve the problem—in the shortest amount of time possible. In his mind, if you have to ask a lot of questions, your credibility could be shaky. An expert should already know most of what's wanted and needed. Asking too many questions could imply that you don't have an immediate answer to his problem. To limit the number of inquiries, your best strategy is to do preresearch.

Be forewarned. There are exceptions to the minimal questions rule with men. A man with an analytical personality will most likely ask you a lot of questions. (In the "Ask Kelly" section, read my answer to "What if the client asks all the questions?")

Another exception occurs when a lot of value has been placed on the end commodity. If the price tag is high, fear or apprehension can be associated with the purchase. A man will then appreciate your asking him questions. This opens the door for him to voice any concerns. It also provides you an opportunity to offer information that can reduce his unease about the risk.

Ask Purposeful Questions

With all customers, a purposeful Discovery Dialogue separates the pros from the beginners. Our B2B seller put much thought into the types of questions asked. The buyer was reassured that the goal was to meet their needs. As a result, they shared lots of information. What a shame about other sellers who try to wing it.

Many people who get into sales or business tend to be action oriented. They are often higher than normal risk takers. If you are a member of the by-the-seat-of-your-pants gang, I urge you to prepare your questions ahead of time. Customers have little patience to wait while you figure out your in-the-moment sales strategy.

Plan Ahead—Not Out Loud

To keep you on track, here are more examples of questions to ask potential buyers. In each scenario, our seller has very specific information to collect. Pay close attention to the *purpose* behind each question.

Example 1: A website designer, working for a business, must collect very detailed information in order to design a customized site. Questions could include: "Tell me about all your products and services." "Are your services in the low, medium, or high price range?" "Describe your typical client, income level, and occupation." "Who's your competition?" "Are you planning to expand in the future?" This information impacts the look, colors, and functionality of a site developed to attract the ideal buyer for the designer's client.

Example 2: A business coach could ask a client, "What are you hoping to achieve from this relationship?" It's not uncommon for people to have unclear or even unrealistic expectations of what a service or product can provide. The next question could be, "Where would you like to see your business in six months, one year, and five years?" Most entrepreneurs and owners of small to midsized businesses have little time to do any advance planning. A great follow-up question would be, "What jobs are you doing now that someone else could do?" A good coach knows that before any new goal can be achieved, something or some things must be taken off a busy client's plate. The answers to all these questions begin to create a blueprint for how the coaching relationship needs to unfold.

Example 3: A retailer selling specialty items such as scuba and deep-sea diving equipment must also choose questions wisely. In such an industry, women often buy equipment for themselves and for others. A good opener to a female customer would be, "Who is the equipment for?" That could be followed with: "For what type of diving?" "Where is the diving done?" "What's the skill level?" Each question narrows down what to show the buyer. It also prevents the seller from making a very common mistake—trying to impress the customer by showing every product from one end of the store to the other, which leads to product information overload. It also causes customers to jump ship before making a purchase!

Planning Pays Off

The quality of each seller's questions demonstrated that they were perfect for the job. The customer's answers then became an easy-to-follow map. The seller was led to a route that few travel—to the sale of the perfect customized solution.

Before you select any question, ask yourself what the buyer's answer will reveal. If the question isn't purposeful, hit the delete button. Take another path. On the following page is a sampling of questions to choose from.

THE 4 W QUESTIONS WITH EXAMPLES

Who   Who is this for?
Who has the problem?
Who needs the solution?
Who else will be using the product/service?

What   What are you looking for?
What problems will this address and/or change?
What do you want this product/service to do for you?
What did you use/do in the past?

When   When was the last time you fixed this?
When was the last time you purchased a similar product/service?
When do you need it?
When do you want to get started?

Where   Where are you using/putting this product?
Where would you like your business to be in five years?
Where in the world did you get that haircut? (Don't really ask that question. I just wanted to see if you were paying attention.)

BONUS QUESTIONS WITH EXAMPLES

How   How often does this situation occur?
How did you hear about us?
How many would you like?
How would you like to pay for this?

Tell me about*

Tell me about your company [staff, locations, business, products, services].
Tell me about yourself [your family, company, situation, ideas].
Tell me about your hopes [dreams, expectations, goals].

*If starting a sentence with "Tell me about . . ." feels too imposing or direct, you can say, "If you don't mind me asking, could you tell me about . . ." or "Just so I understand, could you tell me about . . ."

Ask Kelly

We've covered a lot of important information. However, sellers often have additional questions to ask me—about questions. Some of the most common are here for you, along with my answers.

Seller's Question: How do I keep the conversation on track if it doesn't follow the 1-2-3 questioning sequence?
Kelly's Answer: Let's say you're asking general getting-to-know-you questions and the customer jumps ahead to talk about the solution. Stop. Ask yourself, "Do I know enough about the person and/or company to make recommendations?" If your answer is "No," respond with, "I realize I need to ask a few more questions to really understand your situation [be able to make realistic suggestions]." Then go back to where you left off. It's not uncommon to do this several times during the conversation.

Seller's Question: What if the client asks all the questions?
Kelly's Answer: Fire the client! I'm only kidding. What you're describing is common. "I'd like to know more about [your products/services] . . ." is one of the universal conversation openers (along with "What's the price?" as we discussed earlier).

Your response to an upfront inquiry about your products / services should be a very, very brief answer. Without knowing what the customer really needs, you won't know what to focus on. This is where you can use an "elevator speech" like "I teach people how to have more profitable sales conversations with women and men." (Wait! That's part of what I do. Insert your own mini-description and benefit statement.)

After you give the mini-summary of what you offer, you need to regain control of the conversation. State, "I have a few quick questions to ask. Then I'll fully understand your situation and will know the best solution(s) to recommend to you." Now ask your questions. You may need to use this technique several times throughout the exchange.

Seller's Question: What's the difference between a Discovery Dialogue and a paid Needs Assessment?
Kelly's Answer: Here's the easiest way to differentiate between the two. Consider the Discovery Dialogue as the vehicle which determines why someone would benefit from a Needs Assessment. "Oh, you'd like your business to grow 1,000%, this month! Well, part of our service includes doing a customized Needs Assessment to formulate the best ways to make that happen. First I have a few more questions to ask to understand your situation. What part of your business would you like to grow and for what reasons?"

Seller's Question: Should all my questions be asked in person?
Kelly's Answer: Ideally, whenever you are in front of a potential client, the opportunity to build a relationship increases exponentially. So a face-to-face meeting/conversation would be best. If that's not possible, there are other options.

You can meet virtually over the Internet. More and more sellers use audio/video services such as Skype to speak with customers. Your next choice would be a phone meeting and/or conference call. When companies and organizations contact me for a speaking engagement, our Discovery Dialogues are often held over the phone. Then before my presentation I call preselected participants or e-mail a link to an online survey. This makes it possible to really understand the situation. It also makes it possible for me to customize the session content. By the way, you don't have to be a large company to be able to offer an online survey. There are several easy-to-use online research services, many of which are free. To find them, go to an Internet search engine like Google and type in the key words "free survey."

Seller's Question: In a busy retail environment, what can I ask in ten minutes or less? For example, I sell window coverings in a busy store. People want to see everything on the floor. What are the best questions to ask to zero in on what to show them?
Kelly's Answer: To begin with, I like your approach. Toss out the sales presentation. Focus in on what the customer can really use. This should help you. The following targeted questions make it possible to "zero in on what to show" in under ten minutes!
General Questions: "So that I'll know the type of blinds to show you, I have a few questions to ask." "What room is it for?" "How would you describe the style and color of the room?" "What colors are you considering for the window covering?"
Precise Questions: "Will kids or pets also be using the room? We may need to consider some safety and cleaning options." "How much light do you need to block out, and how big a concern is privacy?"
Focused Questions: "Would you prefer a window covering with slats or a solid piece of material?" "What price range are you looking to spend?"

Seller's Question: When the customer begins with "What's the price?" how should I respond?
Kelly's Answer: You can say, "The price (fee) varies depending on what you are looking for [the work involved, amount

of customization, types of options, number of features]." Then reengage the Discovery Dialogue with, "If you tell me about your situation [what you're looking for, your challenge, what you'd like done, what you'd like improved], then I'll have a better idea of what to suggest."

Seller's Question: What if there isn't a person for me to interview? My accounts put out RFPs. (An RFP is a Request for a Proposal. It requires sellers to submit a written document to describe their product/service, prices, terms, etc.)
Kelly's Answer: Do your homework ahead of time. One of the companies using my OutSell Yourself techniques sells high-tech microscopes. Throughout the year, technical sales reps make informal visits to potential end users. They use the time to ask questions and gather information in advance of the request to submit an RFP.

Another client sells large computer information storage solutions. (Try saying that fast three times!) Instead of trying to sell to every client imaginable, each sales agent targets a specific niche industry. For example, a sales agent will collect info on a specific end-user via sales calls, from reading white papers (reports) and newspapers, and from online forums. This way each learns as much as possible about their potential clientele before the RFPs go out for tender. Yes, it's time-consuming. However, the ROI (return on investment) makes it well worth the effort.

Here's another option. When I did contract training for a large city, I would go to the municipality's RFP Q&A session to gather information. It was amazing how many potential vendors weren't there. It was also amazing how much I learned!

Seller's Question: When selling to couples [or committees], how can I find out the real decision maker?

Kelly's Answer: Let me begin by stressing that you should never make assumptions. Throughout the question-and-answer process, make sure that both people get a chance to share their views. If one remains silent, ask, "So what are your thoughts?" Many sellers have made the mistake of assuming that the person answering all the questions was the real decision maker. By the way, you may or may not find out for certain who'll make the final decision, but all points of view will be on the table to work with. This scenario applies to business situations too.

Here's another approach. Ask, "Would you like a few minutes alone to discuss this?" Most couples will say yes. If they return with, "We talked it over, and thanks—but no thanks," don't give up. You can counter with, "So that I know I served you well, I must ask, do you both feel this way, or is there something I overlooked that's not right for one of you?" Use your Intentional Pause. Look at them individually. Smile and wait. Many members of a couple aren't used to being given personal air time. Someone will often speak up. Initially that person may not have been the decision maker. But similar to the earlier example, they might have an opinion that deserves to be heard—an opinion that can tip the selling scales in your favor. (Remember, under "Precise Questions," you'll find additional examples of how to ask about decision makers and the process.)

Seller's Question: What if someone doesn't know what they want, but asks for a proposal? Recently I asked a client, "What would you like my service to do for you?" They didn't have any idea. So they said, "Write a proposal and I'll look it over." What a huge waste of time. How can I avoid this?

Kelly's Answer: I agree that writing an unfocused proposal is a huge waste of time. Here's the thing. It could be that someone higher up in the company has said, "Get me some quotes," and that's about all the information your buyer has. It could also be that you're dealing with someone who knows they have a problem or wants something to improve. However, they don't have a clue as to how to fix it. That's why they called you. You're the expert.

In both situations, you need to get the buy-in to ask questions. So say, "I know you're busy and don't have time to waste reading long proposals. I just need a few minutes to ask some questions. Then I'll know the best options to recommend."

You can also offer, "I could talk to someone in the company who's directly affected by the problem. Then I'll be able to put together a customized proposal for you. Whom should I call?"

If the next person you speak to also has trouble identifying the real problem, ask, "What would it look like if the situation were to improve?" You might hear something like, "Well, X would work faster" or "Y wouldn't fall apart." You can then translate that feedback into a solution you know would be right for the job without having to write a twenty-page proposal that resembles a short novel . . . which no sane buyer would read anyway.

Seller's Question: My clients give vague answers. How do I find out what they really need? For example, I'm an interior designer. When I ask, "What types of colors do you like?" the client might say "warm." Do they mean pastel warm or earth-tone warm? How can I get them to be more specific?
Kelly's Answer: When you deal with subjective commodities such as colors, patterns, and styles, it's best to use visuals and the process of elimination.

Begin by showing samples. "Example A is a pastel color. Example B is an earth tone." Then ask, "Which do you like the least?" People usually know what they don't want. Then confirm the positive choice and gain their agreement to move forward. "So you like the earth tone the best?" Wait to hear yes.

When selecting from many samples, keep using the process until the exact option is determined. Remember, show extremes and keep narrowing it down with don't-like-it and like-it choices. This may seem time-consuming. However, it's not as time-consuming as dealing with an unhappy client who had a very different interpretation of what they bought. (By the way, this process works in a variety of situations.)

Moving Forward

Asking well-thought-out, open-ended questions made it possible to sell without selling. The quality of your questions built trust and uncovered important information. Your purposeful questions also confirmed to the customer that you are indeed an expert. However, even experts must continually gain the customer's permission to ask questions throughout the sales process. In the next chapter, **"Earn the Right to Proceed**," we'll cover how to do this in detail.

Sell without selling–RECAP

Here's a quick recap of the main points we discussed to Sell without Selling:

Say Good-bye to the Salesperson Act
Customers rarely trust those who try to sound or act like professional sellers. Get rid of any well-rehearsed sales scripts. Ask questions instead.

Have a Discovery Dialogue
Avoid asking closed-end questions that lead to yes or no answers. Use interactive open-ended questions. They are nonthreatening and provide the best insight into your customer's situation and needs.

Keep Your Conversations Flowing
Asking open-ended questions during the Discovery Dialogue enables you to gather three levels of information: general, focused, and precise.

Change Your Questioning Style with Women and Men
Women welcome you to ask enough questions to fully understand their unique situation. With men, you must limit your queries. Men expect you to zero in on solutions more quickly—unless they are considering a commodity with a high level of risk.

Ask Purposeful Questions
Before you speak with a buyer, plan your questions in advance. Ask yourself, "What will the answer to this question reveal?" It is the use of purposeful questions that separates the pros from the beginners.

Ask Kelly

Do not try to guess your way out of situations. Learn from the pros. When in doubt, ask other experts for their help, solutions, and wisdom.

6

Earn the Right to Proceed

Let's admit it. During the sales conversation, most sellers quietly assess the buyer to see if it's a good match. Guess what? The customer does the same thing. Except that someone who's getting ready to open their wallet has a higher set of expectations. After all, they are about to invest money. For this reason, buyers need assurance *throughout* the process that they aren't wasting valuable time talking to you.

You earn permission to move ahead with the sales process when you demonstrate that you have been listening. This seems easy . . . until you're knee deep in a discussion and the customer fires off problems, facts, figures, and buying expectations at the speed of light. Like a dazed traveler about to sink in quicksand, you could be going down fast. But it doesn't have to end this way.

There are easy-to-master communication techniques that keep the conversation flowing, regardless of the circumstances. These tools will boost your credibility and earn you the right to gather information and even to discuss the often gut-wrenching topic known as "What's your budget?" However, as stated before, sellers must first prove that they've been listening.

Listen with Both Ears to Double Your Income

Sellers who listen well can dramatically increase their income. A costly mistake would be to *sort of listen* as the customer provides answers. Not hearing crucial information could result in losing thousands of dollars in sales.

It's not uncommon for sellers to tune out as buyers describe their situation and wants. They're too busy maneuvering in their own heads. Frantically they scheme over which products and services to offer. Regrettably, they miss hearing critical information. Talk about a colossal waste of time and opportunity. Listening to only part of what's being said won't build relationships, gain a buyer's permission to proceed, or pay the bills. *Careful listening* moves the conversation forward. This applies in all sales situations.

Kelly's Keepers

Listening carefully can increase your income.
Sort of listening can cost you sales.

Listen—Listen—Listen

Here's a sales story worth listening to. When writing a recent article, I interviewed a highly successful female account executive who sells communication solutions to large corporations and institutions. Her clients are primarily female CEOs and professionals working in upper-level management. This gal knows how to earn the right to proceed.

In the previous month, she had increased her sales ratio by a whopping 418 percent. Her client retention rate was an outstanding 98.6 percent over five years. I wanted to hear her sales secrets. She shared many. However, the answer that really stood out was her response to "What final advice would you share with sellers?" Her trillion-dollar comeback was, "Shut up and listen." Wow! I couldn't have said it any better myself.

Listening, not imitation, may be the sincerest form of flattery.
DR. JOYCE BROTHERS, PSYCHOLOGIST

Listen Like You Mean It

Too many of us do a horrible job of listening. Don't believe me? Then ask yourself when was the last time someone really listened to you. A time when you weren't interrupted? When you weren't cut off midsentence or put on hold while a friend, family member, or colleague responded to call waiting? Now ask yourself how often you feel fully heard or understood in an average week. Would it be fair to say, "Point made"?

Here's an amazingly basic yet compelling reality. Sellers who fully listen to customers stand out from the majority of their competition. It's a sad fact. But it's true.

Look Potential in the Eye—Once Again

Speaking of how to listen, in chapter 2, "Open Your Mind to Success," we discussed a focusing techique which FM Sellers use to create a high level of verbal self-awareness. FM Sellers intentionally check to see where they're looking when listening to someone. To stay present and in the moment, FM Sellers make it a goal to look customers in the eye, which instantly increases their ability to hear what's being said.

If this practice seems too simplistic, here is some eye-opening information for you. When writing my online column for *Sales & Marketing Management* magazine, I surveyed female entrepreneurs between the ages of 29 and 79. When asked, "What should vendors know when selling to you?" the businesswomen held nothing back. The following is one of many fascinating comments: "Look us in the eye during the sales conversation. Otherwise how will we know you're listening, and how can we trust you?"

Are you kidding me? There are professionals out there who don't have a clue that they've lost a sale because of a lack of eye contact. Well, that can be corrected right now! (Keep in mind that there are exceptions to the look-me-in-the eye request. It's important to research the protocol of your market. In some cultures and religions, making direct eye contact can be taboo.)

Test Your Ability to Listen

There is a simple way to test to assess your ability to focus in and listen to your client. When you leave a Discovery Dialogue, or any conversation for that matter, ask yourself: "What color were the person's eyes? What was their hairstyle? Did they wear glasses? What color was their shirt [jacket, tie, blouse, dress, sweater, t-shirt]?" (Hopefully the person wasn't wearing all those outfits at once. That could be a little distracting.) If you can't answer at least two of the questions, your listening skills still need some work.

Women and Men Want You to Listen—For Different Reasons

One of my PowerPoint slides for an OutSell Yourself presentation shows the photo of a man staring blankly—one would assume at a customer. The audience takes a second or two to gaze back at the fellow. I then say, "To female buyers, this is not considered listening." Men and women laugh aloud as they see their life played out before their eyes. Once the laughter dies down, my next statement gets delivered like a one-two punch: "Surprise—when listening to male buyers, staring blankly won't win you a good seller award either."

Women Need to Be Heard

As I tell audiences, when you have a conversation with all buyers, it's in everyone's best interests to prove that you're listening. With women, your success can hinge on whether or not you communicate that you hear them. When women speak, it releases a chemical in their brain called oxytocin. Considered the feel-good chemical, oxytocin unleashes the desire to connect, trust, and bond. When a woman hears and sees that you're listening, it releases more oxytocin. She feels even better about the sales conversation and about you. As trust builds, the sharing of pertinent information becomes less of a risk. So to fully benefit from the oxytocin experience, you need to hear her out.

Here's a final insight about really listening to a woman. It comes from one of the female entrepreneurs surveyed for the article referred to earlier. Her comment says it all: "Listen and wait until we are finished before answering. Don't just listen to the first part, concoct an answer, and then wait patiently until we are finished to give your answer. You will probably miss the really important detail—the one we slipped in about two-thirds of the way through." Well put!

Men Value Being Heard

Men too respond favorably when they know that they've been heard, but for different reasons than women. As already mentioned, men are goal-oriented. They want to make the best decision, often in the shortest amount of time possible.

Communicating that you have heard them relays the message, "I too see the goal. I am running with you, full steam ahead, to the finish line."

So stop. Take the time to listen. Men will value your demonstration of interest. They will also value your commitment to solving their problems.

Kelly's Keepers
Women need to be heard.
Men value being heard.

Yep, I Really Hear You

With all buyers, you can demonstrate your superb listening skills by using verbal and nonverbal signals. Something as simple as saying, "um," "oh," "ah," or "I see" and nodding your head to indicate "Yes, I hear you" can change everything. It can also show that you're ready, willing, and able to move the sales conversation forward.

There's no genius behind it.
It's persistence and listening to people.
CRAIG NEWMARK, FOUNDER OF CRAIG'S LIST, WWW.CRAIGSLIST.ORG

Do an Expert's Check-In

When sellers fully listen, they can gain a lot of buying respect. They can also hear a mountain of valuable information in a short amount of time. However, when it flies at you that fast, it can feel like a data dump. You could have trouble processing all that the customer has said. If you're positioned as an expert who offers customized solutions, this can be a horrifying prospect.

In an act of desperation, many frantic sellers have tried to pull several strategies out of their sales toolbox. Their goal is to try to decipher complex information, think of the next question to ask, and look intelligent at the same time. Help! Some people will do almost anything to avoid admitting that they are overwhelmed by all the details. Instead of checking in, they'll often resort to guessing what the customer must have meant.

Don't Jump to Conclusions

Experts who make assumptions as to what's been said or what is needed can lose the right to proceed with the sales conversation. Unfortunately, being branded an expert often creates this scenario in the first place. How do you openly admit that you're struggling to keep up with the conversation? That you don't know everything? That you might need something to be clarified or further explained? After all, you're the expert. As the title implies, an expert is expected to know everything. This explains why the most exercise some sellers get is from jumping to conclusions.

Experts Aren't Know-It-Alls

If you identify with being branded an expert who is expected to know everything, here's the same strategy I give consultants to use: Reposition yourself to yourself. Tell yourself that as an expert, you are *not* expected to be a know-it-all. Instead, you are expected to have solid knowledge about your products and services. You are also expected to ask the right questions so that both you and the client will fully understand their situation, their expectations, and the potential solutions. It's not only okay to check in to make sure you understand what's being discussed; as an expert, you are expected to do it.

Experts Check In

Experts check in frequently. To avoid ever having to fake your way through a sales conversation, you can sum up the main points covered during the conversation. Breaking information into bite-sized pieces reduces the chances of overwhelm and misunderstanding. It also earns you the right to proceed. This is reason enough to use one of the best check-in methods known to humankind—paraphrasing.

Kelly's Keepers
Experts check in frequently to confirm understanding.

Experts Paraphrase

To paraphrase properly, recap the main points of your discussion concisely. For example, at various times throughout the Discovery Dialogue, merely restate the *key* things you heard someone say. This confirms to everyone that you understand what was just discussed. If buyers think that something needs clarification or that you missed an important point, they can then correct you. And they often do that . . . when they trust you. Remember, customers also have a stake in making sure that you understand them and their situation.

Paraphrasing can be easier to do than making Thanksgiving dinner. Believe me—I've tried both. However, the majority of sellers unknowingly screw up when they attempt to restate the key points. Instead, they slip into the familiar habit of asking questions to find out more information. Mistakenly, they think they're restating key things. Nope—not even close.

Paraphrasing isn't about asking more Discovery Dialogue questions. Nor is repeating back everything you just heard the client say. That would make you sound like a parrot or appear to be hard of hearing. Instead you simply restate the key things you heard. Below are two different examples of paraphrasing openers.

EXPERT PARAPHRASING STATEMENTS

"So what you're saying is . . ."

"If I understand [you, your role, your family, the situation, the work, your expectations] correctly, you [do the following, require, want, need . . .]."

Experts Practice Until It's Right

Kelly, if I understand you correctly, when I paraphrase, I restate the key points. Then I wait to hear "Yes, that's correct" or "No, that's not correct." To which Kelly responds, "Yes, that's correct."

When you paraphrase, hearing yes earns you the right to proceed. Hearing no earns you the right to re-ask the question until you fully understand. This is what inevitably earns you the right to keep going.

To further demonstrate, we'll use the following example. Let's say you're selling the window coverings from our previous exercise. You and the customer have just discussed many in-depth details related to the general question, "Tell me about the room your window coverings are going into."

In a short amount of time, you have collected so much information that your brain can barely absorb everything. Yet it's all very important to know. Without it, you can't make any customized recommendations. It is vital that you get it right. So now would be the perfect time to do a check-in.

Experts Don't Yak Like a Parrot

To avoid sounding like a parrot, here are some examples of key points you would paraphrase back: "So if I understand you correctly, this is for your living room that's painted mocha-latté brown. Your furniture has an urban-colonial-contemporary look. And your sofa's covered in orange fluffy material. Is this correct?"

If you indeed understood the customer's situation, you would hear yes. If not, the customer can fill in the blanks for you.

It is important to paraphrase only a few points at a time. "If I also understand you correctly, the window covering fabric must be easy to clean because you have twelve children, three dogs, and a hamster. Is this correct?"

"No! I have *three* children, *one* puppy, and *a gerbil*. However, the material still needs to be easy to clean."

Experts Use Paraphrasing to Stand Out

If you're wondering how often you should paraphrase during a conversation, there's no hard and fast rule. However, here's what I suggest: If a lot was discussed and you feel lost in the details—stop. You've just found the best time to paraphrase back the key points. There are situations when I might paraphrase back the key points every few minutes. I do this until it's clear to both the client and to me that I have a solid grasp of the issues and desired outcomes.

If you're concerned that it could annoy customers to hear their conversation repeated back, it doesn't. Customers report that when they rehear the key things they just stated, they feel "heard," "understood," and "more trusting of the seller." This is excellent news. It's now time to get permission to discuss the customer's budget.

Get Permission to Ask about Budgets

Should budget guessing ever become an Olympic sport, the sales team would take home the gold. Even the most experienced sellers can feel dread when it comes time to talk money. When asked, "How many of you would rather be bitten by a rabid dog than have to ask a customer about their budget?" the majority of the professionals I have surveyed would choose the dog bite.

When the same professionals are asked, "So if you don't ask about budgets during the Discovery Dialogue, how do you know which product and service options to suggest?" the most common answer is "I guess." Either too many professionals don't know how to ask about the budget, or they like painful guessing games, or they really like being bitten by rabid dogs.

YOU PLAY THE BUDGET GUESSING GAME WHEN ...

1. You try to read customers' body language to get a sense of how interested they are. If they frown a lot, you'll sell low. If they smile, it's full price.

2. You try to guess how much the customer's watch costs. The more expensive the bling (accessories), the more they'll spend. Unless they wear a designer knock-off watch. In that case, your foolproof plan just bit the dust.

Why Do You Want to Know My Budget?

Before we delve into how to earn the right to discuss a customer's budget, we need to retrace our steps. It's time for an information refresher. In chapter 5, "Sell without Selling," we discussed the important fact that people are more inclined to share information when they know *why* it's in their best interests to do so. This same truth applies to talks about money.

Buyers are more willing to disclose the real budget when they know why revealing that information will benefit them. How you phrase your question will shed light on the budget or it won't. There is no middle ground on this one. You either earn the right to proceed or you don't.

How *Not* to Ask about Budgets

Asking my customers about what they were prepared to spend was a stressful trial and error exercise. I banged my head against the how-to-talk-about-the-budget brick wall more times than I care to admit. During year three of running the sporting goods shops, I finally gathered up enough courage to quit skating around the price issue. (Sorry for the bad sports pun.) That was the year I discovered the two questions that would shut up a customer faster than a clam at an all-you-can-eat seafood buffet.

When selling retail, the first horrible question asked was, "How much do you want to spend?" The reply I often heard was, "I'm not ready to buy. I'm just looking." Where do you go from there?

When discussing a team order, the question that sank faster than a submarine was, "So what's your budget? The popular response to my direct approach was, "Put a quote together and we'll look it over." It only took another six months to realize that probing for an exact budget was a pushy move on my part. The safest thing for the customer to do was to block me out.

How *To* Ask about Budgets

After living through some very frustrating years, it finally dawned on me: Ask for an approximate budget or for price ranges. By dialing back my request, I would lower the commitment a buyer needed to make. It would also earn me the right to hear some numbers. Plus knowing the approximate budget or price ranges would reduce the chances that I'd discount. All of this would ultimately give me room to present several options instead of just one. Break out the noisemakers. It was time to party!

To make double and triple certain I would never again hear, "Why are you asking for my budget?" I began new price discussions with the now-popular statement, "So that I'll know what to recommend . . .? Next I came up with some key questions to follow that statement. Depending on the situation and the buyer, I had a few to choose from:

"What price range are you looking to spend?"

"What's your upper and lower price range?"

"Approximately how much have you budgeted for this?"

The questions worked. When I explained the benefit of supplying the coveted numbers to customers, they were more willing to open up. Words like *price range, upper and lower* range, and *approximately* gave them breathing room. It also provided me the flexibility to offer several solutions within their budget. It became a win-win situation. Fortunately, the same process works today. However, there can be an exception to this rule.

If you come across buyers who have no idea what products or services like yours would cost, you need to educate them before discussing budgets. In such a situation, begin that conversation with, "Typically the fees/prices range from $(low number) to $(high number), and this is what you often get for the money." Then add, "If you tell me which price range seems right for you, we'll have a good starting point."

Kelly's Keepers
Educate buyers unfamiliar with today's prices
before discussing their budget.

During your discussions about approximate budgets, don't be surprised if customers reveal their *exact* budgets. When you had a Discovery Dialogue, not once trying to sell and continually gaining permission to proceed, you built a great relationship and earned a high level of trust. At this point, some buyers will readily cut to the chase and put the real numbers on the table. Whatever the outcome, it's important to know that when discussing the budget, timing is everything.

Timing Is Everything

The best time to talk about money is when you've been given permission to do so. However, that still doesn't address a common recurring concern: When should that happen? Should it be at the beginning, middle, or end of the discussion? There are lots of different opinions about how and when to ask about budgets. So I will throw my thoughts into the mix.

I find it best to broach the money topic toward the end of the Discovery Dialogue. As a reminder, in chapter 5, "Sell without Selling," one of the "Ask Kelly" questions covered a response that you can use if the customer wants to discuss your fees/prices early in the conversation. However, for now, here's my rationale for not talking about budgets after saying hello. It's my policy never to sell anyone on why they should buy from me. In my experience, when a price tag hasn't been attached early in the conversation, people have more freedom to discuss their situation.

For this reason, I ask enough questions so that all issues and potential solutions are known. Then when we do talk money, customers can clearly see the value of investing in my long-lasting solutions. This reduces the knee-jerk reaction of buying the cheapest Band-Aid or quick-fix answer, which customers often regret later on.

From the other side of the sales counter, I use the same purchasing rationale. When I see enough value in something, my credit card whips out so fast that the stock exchange jumps ten points. Wait a minute! Wasn't that the third buying motivator we discussed in chapter 4, "Tap into Your Clients' Buying Motivators"? It's the person, then product and/or service, and finally the price which motivate a customer to buy. Wow, I can't believe I'm that predictable. Oh, well. C'est la vie (that's life)!

A budget tells us what we can't afford,
but it doesn't keep us from buying it.
WILLIAM FEATHER, FOUNDER OF THE *WILLIAM FEATHER MAGAZINE*

Keep Your Reputation Polished

A well-orchestrated Discovery Dialogue, combined with good communication skills, gives fantastic insight into what the customer needs. However, even if you and the client hit it off, there can be situations when it is obvious that your solution may not be the right fit for them or their budget. No matter how lucrative the sale may appear, it's not worth it to compromise your good name, goodwill, and ability to get ongoing referrals. Don't waste their time or yours trying to fit a square peg into a round hole. Be an expert and call in other experts. Refer the buyer to someone else. This frees you to work with your perfect customer. And who knows—another seller could be referring a client to you!

Our ultimate freedom is the right and power to decide how any-
body or anything outside ourselves will affect us.
STEPHEN COVEY, AUTHOR OF *PRINCIPLE-CENTERED LEADERSHIP*

Important Update!

As if to prove my point, one hour after I wrote the "Keep Your Reputation Polished" information, an e-mail arrived from a past client. She was looking for an expert to speak on a specific topic. The subject matter was different from my own. So why did she contact me? There could be several reasons.

Here are a few theories. I have a good performance record with the organization, and she values my input. It could be because I have access to other top-level experts. I'm a past president of the Toronto Chapter of the Canadian Association of Professional Speakers (CAPS) and a member of the National Speakers Association (NSA). Or she could simply be in a bind. Whatever her reason, the point is that she trusted me enough to recommend another professional, which I did.

In the old days, I would have considered trying to reinvent myself in a heartbeat. The midnight oil could have burned away as I labored to become the topic expert she wanted. After all, work was work, or so I thought. However, it only took one very uncomfortable experience of overpromising and underdelivering to eliminate that thinking quickly.

Today I operate with the certainty that being an expert means knowing what you excel at. It also means knowing when it's in everyone's best interests to make an expert referral. The law of cause and effect reminds us all that what goes around comes around. How we respond to any situation lets us choose what that outcome will be. I choose to earn the right to proceed, when it's best for both me and the client. That's what I choose.

Moving Forward

When you demonstrated that you really understood your buyer, you earned the right to proceed and discuss their budget. The sales process continues to flow. You are now ready to **Lead with Your Best Solution.**

EARN THE RIGHT TO PROCEED—RECAP

Here's a quick recap of the main points we discussed to Earn the Right to Proceed:

Listen with Both Ears to Double Your Income
Sellers who fully listen to customers stand out from the majority of their competition, and that can pay off.

Women and Men Want You to Listen—For Different Reasons
Women need to be heard. Men value being heard.

Do an Expert's Check-In
Real experts drop the know-it-all label. They check in with clients to confirm their understanding of all the details.

Get Permission to Ask about Budgets
Customers who know why it's in their best interests to disclose budget information are more comfortable doing so, especially when asked about their approximate budget.

Keep Your Reputation Polished
Your solution may not be the right fit for every customer. Be the expert who knows when to make an expert referral.

7

Lead with Your Best Solution

Everything you've done has taken you to this exact point. Trust
has formed between you and the buyer. You've learned a lot about
their situation, needs, and expectations. Plus you know the price
range they'll spend for your solutions. All of this happened with
ease, in a short time. You're now at the perfect place to lead with
your best product and service solutions. The great part is that not
once did you have to sell. So why start now?

A curious thing happens when it's time to talk solutions. Even
the most enlightened person can feel the fear of not getting the
sale creep in. Talk about a defining moment. Do you take the FM
Seller (Focused Manifester) success route: "I am ready, willing,
and able"? Or will you lose faith and follow the AM Seller (Aimless Manifester) path to the dead-end street known as "If I don't
push to close this sale, I won't be able to pay my bills."

Feature Your Benefits

To stop yourself in your tracks, before fear has you selling any old
solution, you must remind yourself why you and your products
and services are worth the money. As demonstrated in chapter 2,

131

"Open Your Mind to Success," and chapter 3, "Unleash Your Real Value," it's your positive thoughts and your thoughtful planning which fuel your ability to connect to the successful outcomes you wish to attract.

> *You will either step forward into growth*
> *or you will step back into safety.*
> ABRAHAM MASLOW, PSYCHOLOGIST

So before you put any solutions and prices together, why not continue to strengthen your success-fueled mindset? It will leave little room for the fear of failure. The surest way to feel good about what you offer is to gain clarity about the benefits of your solutions.

Feature and Benefits Are Different Animals

This may come as a surprise to some people. Just as you might feel unsure about how great your solutions are, the buyer may have similar concerns. Customers may be attracted to the features of what you offer, but it's the benefits of your products and services that really win them over. If you mistakenly focus on the bells and whistles, you could lose out.

When you define the benefits of your goods, not only will you be convinced of the value of what you offer, but so will your buyer. Before we go any further, we need to make sure that we are speaking the same sales language. Sellers often confuse features with benefits. If we don't clear this up, the rest of what's here for you might not make sense.

- Features are what a product/service has. (Yawn . . .)
- Benefits are the value buyers get from the features. (Now you're talking!)

For example, a pen comes with a cap (feature). The cap fits over tip of the pen (ho hum). The cap (feature) stops the ink from drying out (big benefit). The cap (feature) also stops the ink from staining your clothes so you can look great all day long (even bigger benefit—where can I buy a dozen?!).

When you asked precise questions like "What would you like this product or service to do for you?" and "How will you measure the success of this solution?" the answers you heard were the *benefits* your customer was after: "I want our company to save money" or "I want the window coverings to be easy to clean . . . because I have three children, one puppy, and a gerbil."

Remember, customers don't just buy features. They *invest* in the benefits. They look for the WIIFM factor—What's In It For Me? So before you suggest any buying options, first identify the benefits of your products and services. This will increase your selling confidence and your customer's buying confidence.

What WIIFMs Do You Offer?

The following exercise shows you how to identify the benefits of your products and services. For every feature you write down, simply ask yourself "So what?" just as your customer would. The answer reveals the benefits of that feature. Speaking of benefits, do this exercise and you'll have a great benefit list in less time than it takes to toast a loaf of bread.

FEATURE	BENEFIT
(List your feature.)	(Answer the question "So what?")
Turbo-Booster Toaster toasts bread 700% faster than a conventional toaster.	More time to sleep in—even on workdays!

The Benefit of Benefits

With your benefit list complete and all those feel-good endorphins surging through you, we're about to kick this conversation up ten notches. It's time to discuss how a customer links those same WIIFM benefits to the decision-making process.

To make the best buying choice, a customer establishes criteria by which to make decisions. Think of these desired benefits as a wish list or checklist. Whether purchasing a product such as a jar of peanut butter or hiring a service expert, the customer compares the benefits of your goods and services against their wish list. This makes it possible to determine if something has enough WIIFMs and is a good ROI (return on their investment).

Benefits Sell Products

Buyers compare the benefits of each product against their wish list. For example, when standing in front of several jars of peanut butter, a savvy shopper might mutter, "I could buy a fourteen-gallon jar of BIG Nutty Buddy Peanut Butter. It should last three months. Plus I love that Smiling Peanut guy on the label. Oh, there's a sixteen-ounce jar of Crunchy Munchy Peanut Butter. But I'd finish it in a week. I hate running out of peanut butter. So fourteen gallons

134

of BIG Nutty Buddy Peanut Butter will be perfect!" (Big jar, big what's-in-it-for-me benefit, big return on investment!)

In that example, it's important to recognize that our customer's ROI criteria weren't based on price. I've said it before, and I'll say it again: "Price isn't the number one buying motivator." Nope. Not even close.

Our customer had a very different buying motivator in mind. They hated to shop. Therefore, it was of great benefit to purchase a huge jar of peanut butter. This is the kind of information you'd find out only during the interactive Discovery Dialogue when asking, "So, how often do you like to buy peanut butter?" These are wish-list needs you can only meet when you understand the true benefits of what your product offers.

Benefits Sell Services Too

The same principles apply when selling services. As an expert in sales, I must offer solutions loaded with WIIFM benefits—that is, if I want to get business. For example, the decision makers typically look for something to be improved, such as increasing sales in a shorter length of time. So it doesn't make sense to blab on about a generic feature such as, "My program shows professionals how to have a Discovery Dialogue." So what?

For that reason, once I identify the benefits of each of the OutSell Yourself selling skills (features), I'm better able to link them to the client's decision-making criteria. Now the conversation becomes: "Replacing your company's sales presentation with a Discovery Dialogue makes it possible to find out exactly what your customer wants (great benefit). This will ultimately free up time to speak with more clients and increase sales (huge benefits—huge WIIFM)."

In a decision maker's eyes, the benefits match their distinct needs. And they convert into an excellent return on investment! Simply put, my OutSell Yourself sessions and keynote presentations become the BIG Nutty Buddy of sales training.

But don't think that I leave anything to chance. Before putting my proposal together, I involve the client in helping to decide the best solutions (WIIFM benefits) to offer them. The goal is to eliminate any guesswork. My solutions must always match up with the client's wish list.

Kelly's Keepers
Customers look for WIIFMs (What's In It For Me?).
Speak about the benefits of what you offer.

Let the Customer Help Write the Proposal

Before any proposal goes out, it's given a test run. During a brief discussion with the client, I go over the proposed benefits. The goal is to make sure that I've got it right. Some of you may be shaking your heads in amazement. Could this be true? Yes! My clients help me to select the perfect solutions for them. These winning solutions are absolutely in sync with their own buying criteria. Don't be fooled, though. This wouldn't be possible if a high level of buying trust hadn't first been established—then maintained throughout the sales conversation. So let's go for it.

Within the problem lies the solution.

AUTHOR UNKNOWN

Explore with Your Buyer

When you explore a product or service solution, it's best to remind the client of what has been discussed so far. It's vital to do this when a lot of information has been covered. You're not the only one who can get lost in the details.

"Based on my understanding that you're looking for [describe the benefit] an easy-to-clean window covering because you have [name the problem, situation, desired outcome] three children, one puppy, and a gerbil, here are some options to consider . . ."

Now we'll break this statement down. We started with "based on *my understanding . . .*" It's best to avoid saying "because *you* said…" Even though they said it, not everyone wants to take full responsibility for making the final decision. What if they agreed to the wrong solution? What if you or your solutions aren't as great as promised? Ultimately, they'd take the heat—not you.

We also said, "Here are some options to consider . . ." The words *some, options,* and *consider* lower the commitment that you're asking the buyer to make. It also reassures them that it's not yet time to make a final decision. The statement says, "We're just exploring the possibilities so that we can fully customize the solutions." It also confirms that there is no pressure to buy.

When in Doubt—Ask

Whenever you make any type of suggestion, you must determine if you're on track. Otherwise, how will you know if your proposed solutions make sense to the buyer? How will you know if your idea is good enough to move forward and put into a quote? Maybe you need to keep probing to find the perfect options. When in doubt, just ask the customer. Here are a few ways to do that.

JUST ASK THE CUSTOMER

1. "What are your thoughts?"

2. "Are we on the right track?"

3. "Are these suggestions moving us in the right direction?"

"It's Okay—I Guess"

When you check in to see if the proposed solutions are on track, you could let loose a variety of responses. You might hear "yes," "no," "maybe," "sort of," or "it's okay, I guess." Yes, of course, means that your ideas are on the money. Great! You can proceed to write up the proposal and collect your money. If, however, you heard no, don't give up. Respond with "Good to know. What would work better for you?"

If the customer gives an uncertain response such as "It's okay, I guess," keep probing. Don't stop until you're fully satisfied that your suggestions are right on. The following fictional conversation demonstrates how to do an in-depth needs inquiry.

Situation: You have suggested a service that you think could meet the customer's needs. The client leans back in the chair, crosses their arms, and vocalizes a lukewarm reaction to your proposed solution. Oh, I should mention, this customer's not a big talker. Now you have an even bigger challenge on your hands. But don't worry; you will handle the situation like the pro you are!

Inquiry Conversation:
Seller: "So what do you think about the service as described?"
Buyer: "It's okay, I guess."
Seller: "What part of it is okay?"
Buyer: "The first part."

Seller: "Just to be clear, are you referring to…?"

Buyer: "Yep."

Seller: "What can we change, add, or do differently so that it works for you?"

Buyer: "I'd want it to do A and B. C isn't important to me."

If you were our fictional seller, I would say, "Well done! You probed until the right solution appeared. Also by encouraging the customer to think about the benefits they wanted from your solutions, you helped them to establish firm criteria by which to make their final buying decisions. What an amazing strategy you used! Your sales coach is very proud of you. You're more than ready to put your quote together."

When I've got pressure on me, I don't panic.
I look for the right solution, and then I go for it.
MAGIC JOHNSON, BASKETBALL SUPERSTAR

Say Good-bye to Take-It-or-Leave-It Options

My father unknowingly taught me some important sales lessons. For example, when you put together your formal written or verbal quotes, you need to offer *several* buying options. Great advice—thanks, Dad!

My Dad Could Sell Snow to Eskimos

The reason Dad understood the value of offering options was because the man could sell anything. During his working life, Pops had been a traveling salesman. He later went on to own partnerships in several businesses. However, most of what he passed on to me occurred long before I ever opened my first business. You see, my father didn't use parenting skills with me and my siblings. He used selling skills. And he was good!

Here's a sample of what we heard in my house: "Okay, kids, I have two options for you. You can go to bed now or in five minutes. What'll it be?" Yes, my Dad knew that providing options would keep his young clients happy, and it would also make his life bearable. In hindsight, this was a great lesson for me to learn—which I have put to good use.

Offering several buying solutions can ward off many problems. Yet too many professionals offer just one price, one product, or one service package. That's so unfortunate. The one-solution quote often closes the door on further discussion with a variety of buyers. So Dad, you certainly got that one right!

The 50/50 Gamble

In business, when you give only one buying option, it's like shouting, "Here it is! Take it or leave it." Talk about a 50/50 gamble. Even if you preface it with "If this doesn't meet your needs, just let me know," you're still taking a big risk. What if you suddenly found out that a committee would be making the final decision? Maybe a previously unidentified family member, or anyone else you didn't speak to directly, suddenly appeared. These people wouldn't have any idea of what else you could offer. Regrettably, your one-solution package couldn't give them any insights either.

If those true-to-life scenarios aren't compelling enough to justify offering several buying options, here are a few more to consider. Let's start with the reality that you could meet buyers who only make a decision after they compare one option against another. No matter how great your product or service appears, the buying verdict comes down to "How will I know it's the best solution out there?"

Give Women What They Really Want

Women are a perfect example of the buyers who weigh the pros and cons of one option again another. When women make buying decisions, they use what I refer to as the **Comparative Choice Method**. Even if a woman feels that a product or service will meet her needs, the final selection is based on how it compares to something of similar value. This isn't because women are fussy, as some sellers have misinterpreted. It's because women are big-picture thinkers.

On average, women consider almost double the number of buying factors that men consider. They assess a purchase against its ability to stand the test of time. How it'll meet the needs of those around them. Whether there are enough benefits to justify the cost. Finally, how it compares to what else is out there.

Women Will Tell You Their Buying Criteria—If You Listen

If you listen carefully to women, you'll hear everything that makes up their buying criteria. So why go to all the effort to build a buying relationship, find out those needs, and then present only one solution? That's crazy. Women shop by comparison. So give them what they want. Give them something to compare. If you don't, you just handed them an engraved invitation to check out the competition.

Look through the Eyes of a Top Decision Maker

What if you sell to companies? Your proposal could end up in the hands of a decision maker with several quotes to compare. To further illustrate how self-defeating it can be to offer only one buying option, we'll bring back our business-to-business seller from our B2B case study in chapter 5, "Sell without Selling." To refresh your memory, it was the seller who asked all three levels of Discovery Questions, whose identity will now be revealed: She is the world renowned executive coach Martha Mind-Matters.

In this scenario, CEO and top decision maker Nick Claus from the Gifts Galore Company has asked Martha to send in a written proposal. Nick is about to compare Martha's quote against competitor Frank Smart-Guy's quote.

Which Proposal Grabs Your Buying Attention?

Here's the scene: It's Monday morning. As the head honcho, Nick has twenty-seven e-mails to answer, three internal personnel fires to put out, and a full voice mailbox to deal with. Oh, and then there's the decision on who to hire to do the job. Two proposals sit side by side on his desk. I invite you to look at them too. Then ask yourself which one grabs your buying, or buy-in, attention and why?

Smart Guy Consulting Group

Attn: Nick Claus, Gifts Galore Company
488 Rudolph Lane, Suite 100-7000
North Pole, 20347

To Whom It May Concern:

Based on our combined three years of expertise in the field of executive management coaching and our recent track record of achieving results, we recommend the following to meet your needs.

• Management Turnaround Session

• $10,500 + (plus travel, accommodations, and photo copies)

We look forward to hearing from you.

Sincerely,

Frank Smart-Guy
President-Consultant-Coach-Speaker-Workshop Leader-Blog
Writer-Change Agent-Visionary-Solution Distributor-Podcaster

Mind-Matters Consulting Network

Attn: Nick Claus, Gifts Galore Company
488 Rudolph Lane, Suite 100-7000
North Pole, 20347

Dear Nick,

Based on my understanding that your organization seeks to improve the following management skills:

- Ability to increase efficiency by assigning personality-specific jobs
- Ability to reduce errors by improving verbal communication

The following options are customized for your consideration.

Option 1:
- Customized Skill-Building Session (outline & objectives attached)
- Two follow-up group phone coaching sessions (outline & objectives attached)
- Individual coaching session for senior manager (outline & objectives attached)

Investment: $18,400 (travel & accommodations extra)

Option 2:
- Customized Skill-Building Session (outline & objectives attached)

- One follow-up group phone coaching session (outline & objectives attached)

Investment: $14,700 (travel & accommodations extra)

Option 3.
- Customized Skill-Building Session (outline & objectives attached)

Investment: $11,800 (travel & accommodations extra)

As discussed, I will call tomorrow at 1:00 p.m. to answer any questions, confirm if these options fit, or determine if other packages would better meet your needs. In the meantime, please feel free to contact me if you have questions or are ready to proceed.

Best regards,

Martha Mind-Matters
Executive Coach

(Don't use the fees in either example. They're fictitious.)

The Verdict

If you're like most decision makers, you would have paid close attention to Martha Mind-Matters' proposal. Here's why. She presented three terrific options. She also attached an outline summarizing the objectives (benefits).

If you didn't hire her immediately, chances are good that you would at least follow up with her. Good old Martha had many significant door-opening elements in her quote—all of which centered on the **4 Steps to a Great Written Proposal** formula and **Kelly's Rule of 20s,** which we'll now discuss.

4 Steps to a Great Written Proposal

Every good proposal has a solid structure. Whether you sell computer solutions, adventure vacations, or anything in between, there are four key steps to developing a great proposal. They are:

1. Don't tell clients what they need.
2. Remind clients of problems to be solved and desired outcomes.
3. Present customized options.
4. Use proactive calls to action.

To demonstrate each step, Martha's and Frank's quotes were put under the sales microscope. The following is a dissection of both quotes. As you review the next section, keep in mind that the four-step quotation format, which Martha used, can be applied to both verbal and written proposals. You merely change the vocabulary you use when speaking to women and to men. For specific examples of how to turn the format into a face-to-face presentation, go to the section below entitled "Give Boring Face-to Face Presentations the Heave-Ho." Then check out the piece on "Change Your Delivery with Women and Men." For now, let's continue our assessment of the quotes.

Step One: Don't Tell Clients What They Need

Martha did a terrific job when she opened with the now-familiar statement, "Based on my understanding [that your company seeks to improve the following management skills . . .]." Martha didn't tell the client what they needed; she restated her understanding of the Discovery Dialogue. This served two important purposes. If for any reason Martha had misunderstood or misinterpreted the customer's needs, she kept the door open to offer a better alternative. Customers will often allow a seller to do this . . . if the person hasn't tried to sell them.

Another upside of not telling buyers what they need relates directly to the accountability factor. As mentioned earlier, even though the client did tell Martha about their problems, many buyers are squeamish about being held accountable, especially in print, for buying decisions. That's why it's best that you take on the responsibility of interpreting what the customer needs.

Kelly's Keepers
Open a proposal with
"Based on my understanding . . ."

Step Two: Remind Clients of Problems to Be Solved and Desired Outcomes

Martha scored even bigger points when she reminded the client of the problems she was solving and the desired outcomes: "Based on my understanding that your organization seeks to improve the following management skills . . . ability to increase efficiency by assigning personality-specific jobs . . . ability to reduce errors by improving verbal communication . . ."

Restating the problem and desired outcomes also averted a potentially disastrous outcome. Even though Martha had discussed the client's situation two days ago, checked in to confirm her understanding of their problems and what they wanted to improve, and then worked with the client to find the best solutions, a funny thing happened. The client talked to two other potential vendors who had many other solution ideas. Next the decision maker met with four associates and ran all ideas past them. Suddenly the situation had changed. As a result, Martha's proposal risked being out of date. Her services were potentially obsolete.

To keep everyone focused, Martha restated the problems and anticipated results that her proposal addressed. This way, if things were to change, the customer would be aware that they were no longer comparing apples to apples. They could ask Martha to quote on a jar of applesauce. They'd know to do this because when Martha provided three options and restated the problem and outcomes that her options could handle, it positioned her as an expert. The implied message was, "If these solutions don't meet your needs, I have the ability to further customize until the perfect solution is found." This is an important distinction that Frank's one-option quote didn't deliver.

Kelly's Keepers
Always restate the problem(s) your solution will solve.

Step Three: Present Customized Options

Your proposal stands out, in a good way, when you present customized options. The detail in your customized options makes it easier for a buyer to see how the solutions are a perfect fit. Poor old Frank Smart-Guy didn't get it. His one generic option was a total bust—for many reasons.

Besides offering only one solution, Frank didn't outline the purpose of that option or its benefits. He neglected to focus on the WIIFMs, so how could the customer assess if it was a good solution? Frank's one-size-fits-all program also relayed this message: "I'm a generalist. If you don't find what you're looking for, I'm really sorry."

Good old Martha Mind-Matters got it right again with her three-option quote. What a good listener and high achiever! This gal's true FM Seller material.

Kellys Keepers
Customized options solve problems.
They also make it easier for buyers to justify investing money.

Step Four: Use Proactive Calls to Action

The final important component of a great proposal is proactive calls to action. Should I call you? Will you call me? Frank left himself in a lurch with the closing statement "We look forward to hearing from you." Those seven simple words just declared that voice mail war was about to begin. A good closing sentence contains three proactive calls to action:

A. Your commitment to follow up [I'll call you . . .]

B. The reassurance that you are the perfect choice [I'll answer questions . . . I'll put together other packages . . .]

C. An invitation for the client to contact you [In the meantime, please feel free to contact me if you have questions or are ready to proceed.]

Kellys Keepers
End with proactive calls to action:
"I'll call you [date and time] . . .
in the meantime, you call me if you [have questions . . .]"

When you present a proposal in person, it's also vital to establish calls to action. In chapter 8, "Listen to Hear Yes," you'll find many examples of such proactive actions in the section called "Stand Back as the Customer Asks to Buy."

Whether your proposal is written or verbal, I'll now show you in detail how Martha priced, packaged, and presented her buying solutions. This will ensure that your sale also unfolds naturally.

Bottom-Up Pricing Doesn't Float

Another plus for Martha Mind-Matters was that she didn't use the all-too-common bottom-up pricing. This occurs when a seller presents the cheapest option first. Those who use bottom-up pricing do so for several reasons. Unfortunately, their misguided thinking dumps the organic flow of working with the client straight into the composter.

Some sellers think that offering the cheapest solution first will open the door to be able to upsell the customer. Upselling is a technique in which the seller attempts to encourage the customer to purchase more expensive items, upgrades, or other add-ons. I use the word *encourage* very loosely.

When upselling, many sellers often have a hidden agenda—to make the sale more profitable. Then there are other sellers who think that by offering a cheaper alternative first, they won't scare off the buyer. Sadly, both theories are full of holes.

Here's the first problem. When presented with the cheapest option first, it's tough for a customer to shift gears. In the buyer's mind, it's been established that the no-frills package will do the job—or most of it anyway. Their internal conversation becomes very bottom-line: "This should do." To then justify paying for premium solutions doesn't make sense. Most buyers would have to feel very deserving to turn around and rationalize adding on features and paying more money.

Put yourself in the same situation. What would it take to convince yourself that it's worth spending the really big bucks for premium goods? Especially after you just sold yourself on how the lower-priced stuff was adequate value for money. This selling theory stinks.

It Can't Be That Good—Not for That Price

There's another situation where bottom-up pricing can come back to haunt you: selling to the customer who's willing to pay good money for the best solution. They came to you because they had a problem or need that they want addressed correctly. They aren't looking for a no-frills patch job. In my experience, this buyer is very wary of low prices or deals.

Fees and prices create perceptions. A frequent misperception in the buyer's mind is that lower fees translate into getting lots—cheap. Nothing could be further from the truth. Low prices don't necessarily imply lots of stuff for the money. Low prices often imply a lack of experience on the part of the seller, inferior goods, or inferior quality.

Buyers who hire experts or want premium goods don't just turn and walk away from this scenario. They often run in the opposite direction. Almost everyone has a you-get-what-you-pay-for horror story. Who wants to relive that nightmare? A seller's best course of action is to use a pricing strategy that enables them to present several purchase options, highlighting the best option first, as Martha did.

Use Kelly's Rule of 20s to Formulate Prices and Packages

Martha Mind-Matters used Kelly's Rule of 20s to fine-tune her three selling solutions. As you saw in her quote, Martha presented three options. Each package had a different number of features and benefits, which corresponded to the price. The price spread between each package was approximately 20 percent. (She rounded the numbers off.)

To keep everything in a logical flow, she presented the premium package first. After all, her Discovery Dialogue uncovered many needs. It only made sense to demonstrate, right up front, that she could meet *all* of those needs.

Below you'll find a visual example of how all the pieces fit together. Included are a client's typical responses.

Option 1 - $18,400
    1. Feature - Benefit
    2. Feature - Benefit
    3. Feature - Benefit

"Must-Have!" Option
    Provides a longer-term solution

Option 2 - $14,700
    1. Feature - Benefit
    2. Feature - Benefit

"It's Okay" Option
    Has most of what the client needs

Option 3 - $11,800
    1. Feature - Benefit

"If I Have To" Option
    Fixes a short-term problem or meets an immediate need

When presented with three options, from top to bottom, the buyer's internal dialogue sounds something like this: "Wow, option one has everything I want. Umm, option two has most of what I want. Then there's option three. It's so basic. It'll do, if need be."

Kelly's Keepers
Present prices from the top to the bottom.

Because packages one and two have similar options in fairly close price ranges, buyers often ignore the lowest-priced package. Instead, they compare the features and benefits of option one against option two. If they are in a position to purchase the premium solution, that's great. If their budget says otherwise, they've still made a good buying decision with option two.

However, if the buyer has limited funds to work with, option three will solve an immediate problem. The best news is that you were able to provide a solution without discounting your prices to get the sale.

Kelly's Keepers
Offer options to fit different budgets;
you will never have to discount.

Now that we've covered how to put together a great written proposal, I'll show you how to deliver the same client-focused proposal in person.

Give Boring Face-to-Face Presentations the Heave-Ho

You may do face-to-face presentations or give quotes over the phone. In each case, after you've worked with the customer to narrow down the options, you can use the same 4 Steps to a Great Proposal formula to format your quote.

4 Steps to a Great Face-to-Face Presentation

The following outlines each step of how to prepare and deliver a quote in person. This includes examples of what to say or not to say.

1. Don't tell clients what they need.

"You really should get this—today." (Eliminate all high-pressure statements like this from your vocabulary.)

2. Remind clients of problems to be solved and desired outcomes.

"Based on my understanding that you're looking to [solve, improve, increase, decrease…] the following…"

Or:

"It sounds to me that you'd like to [solve, improve, increase, decrease . . .] the following . . ."

3. Present customized options.

"Here are three options to consider. Let's start with the one that meets all your needs. It has X, Y & Z that will do the following [meet your need for] . . .

The next option is . . . and it will meet your need for . . . However, it doesn't do [have, include] . . .

Finally, there's a third option which will meet your need for . . ." (Don't mention what this option won't do or what it doesn't include. This choice is so basic that it's obvious it'll only meet one or two needs.)

4. Use proactive calls to action. (Examples are in chapter 8 under "Stand Back as the Customer Asks to Buy.")

Change Your Delivery with Women and Men

When you deliver your product and service solutions to women and to men, know that each responds differently to your verbal approach. There are words and phrases that you'll want to change for each gender. But first you need to know why.

Women Want Tailored Solutions

To a woman, the buying process tends to be personal. For example, before shopping or calling a vendor, a woman will often ask others for referrals. Then before meeting with a buyer, most women will do prebuying research to get up to speed on the proposed solutions.

Women Want a Made-to-Order Conversation

As discussed in chapter 5, "Sell without Selling," during the sales conversation, a woman will want to explain her unique situation. She'll expect the seller to listen and ask questions that pertain to her situation. So it stands to reason that the delivery of buying solutions should be personalized as well.

It is best to use the words *you* and *your* in the conversation, as was demonstrated in the example for giving a face-to-face quote: "Here are three options for you to consider. Let's start with the one that meets all your needs."

Next, link your suggestions directly to the needs she expressed: "It has X, Y & Z that will do the following for you [your team, your company, meet your need for] . . ."

Whether buying for her work or home, a woman invests of herself to make good buying decisions. When discussing options, you move forward when you speak with her and not at her. So personalize your solutions when selling to a woman.

Men Want Proven Solutions

As we have noted throughout the book, men have a different buying process from women. Because men are goal oriented and want to find the best solution in the shortest amount of time, they'll often try to solve a problem on their own first. If they can't find a solution, they'll then ask for help. When they do seek out help, they'll turn to an expert—someone they expect will offer proven solutions. When talking about product and service solutions with a man, you may need to adjust your style to be most effective.

The Way He Drives Says It All

Think about the age-old story of the couple driving. It illustrates what we are talking about. A husband and wife are taking a cross-country vacation. On the second day, after going in circles, the wife turns to her husband, who is behind the wheel, and says, "Honey, I'm sure that we're lost. Shouldn't we stop and ask for directions?" Confidently he replies, "No, I can figure this out." Three blocks later she asks, "Shouldn't we at least look at a map?" With a little less assurance in his voice, he stammers, "No, I really do think I've figured it out now." After turning the corner, only to land at a street they were just on, hubby finally concedes.

Leaning his head out of the car window, he shouts to a local standing on the corner, "Hi, where's the nearest entrance to get to the freeway?" With the authority of a well-traveled expert, the local responds, "Oh, you can't miss it. Just follow those blue signs hiding behind the big trees." Smiling, the husband turns to his wife and says, "I knew I'd figure it out."

Based on the lessons in the story, keep in mind that when you present solutions to a male buyer, he probably wasn't able to solve the problem on his own or may have lacked the right resources to do so. He's now turned to you, the expert in your industry. He expects you to have dealt with similar situations. He also expects that you will apply those proven strategies to solve his problem. When you solve the problem, he'll often take credit for it. After all, in his mind he was expert enough to consult with another expert.

He Wants You to Sound Like an Expert

You'll gain credibility with statements that reassure that others have benefited from these solutions too. "Well if I were you, I'd use . . ." or "Here's what someone in your same situation bought." You could also say, "We've dealt with this before. We did this and this, and we got this result. And we can do this and this for you." However you frame your wording, make sure to link your credibility statements to the options he needs. It's also vital to give him several options to choose from, as Martha Mind-Matters' excellent proposal proved.

Kelly's Keepers

Offer personalized solutions to women
and proven solutions to men.

As you've just seen, the method for doing a verbal presentation is very straightforward. Simply change what you *emphasize* when speaking to a woman and to a man. Offer personalized solutions to women and proven solutions to men. By the way, when speaking to a couple, you can apply a similar strategy. Just combine the techniques: "I am suggesting this option for you because it meets your need for X, Y, & Z, and it has worked successfully in situations similar to yours."

The only thing left to cover is how to talk about your prices—without throwing up.

Discuss Your Price—Without Throwing Up

When you present buying options in person, at some point you have to open your mouth to spew out your prices. The logical time to talk money is *after* you've restated your understanding of the problem and desired outcomes, then described each option and the benefits it provides. Unfortunately, talking about money often engages the gag reflex. I'm sorry to say that there's no way to get around talking about money. Believe me, many sellers have tried.

Some people scribble numbers on napkins or sticky notes, then pass the bad news to the customer to try to decipher. Others pretend to talk to their manager. Somehow, it seems easier to present prices from a fictional cutthroat boss.

Then there are sellers who initially mention low prices to create comfort for everyone. When the excited buyer says yes, the bomb drops: "Oh, I should mention that for your flooring to have the Ever-Glow finish, it's another $900. The two-tone colors are an additional charge. Then there are the delivery, installation, and clean-up fees. Those charges will of course be added to the final total. However, the base product itself has the lowest price you'll find anywhere."

What's Up?

Give me a break! All of these strategies simply turn the relationship back into a sale. The buyer is now on guard, thinking, "I knew it. They were out to make a sale."

A seller earns a lot of buying trust with an open communication style. The buyer expects that same person to expertly guide them through the final decision-making process. Be the seller who's consistent.

Personalizing Your Price—Bracing for the Blow

"Kelly, I'm ready to submit my quote to a customer. But I'm really nervous about talking about my prices. Could I practice with you?"

"Sure. Go for it."

Seller (pretending to sell):

"Hello, Ms. McCormick. I've put together three prices and an attractive package to meet your needs."

Coach Kelly (pretending to be client):

"All righty, let's hear what you've got."

Seller (pretending to sell):

"Well I . . . I can do X, Y, and Z for you." [Pause . . . cough . . . throat clearing . . . pause.] "I charge . . . [pause . . . cough . . . throat clearing . . . pause] $70 an hour." [Long pause—at least three seconds.] "If that's too much money, umm, ah, well, I could give you a discount!"

Role-Playing Autopsy

Well, well, well. Several significant things contributed to this sales call falling apart, besides not providing options and offering a discount that the buyer hadn't even asked for. The amount of pausing and throat clearing done before, during, and after stating the price was a dead giveaway of how obviously uncomfortable the seller was.

The bargain hunter will quickly jump in to take advantage of even the slightest indication of insecurity on the part of the seller.

In this case, they just walked in on a potential going-out-of-business sale. Buyers who hire experts will lose confidence in this seller and their solutions faster than you can say "Next." Sadly, it was all because something very minor contributed to the seller's insecurity. Something that most sellers aren't even aware of—it's the turn of the *phrase* used to describe their prices.

There's Power in Your Words

Using pronouns like "*I* charge" and "*my* fee is" can cause even the most hardened seller to feel queasy. The words also imply that *your* fee is subjective. *You* made the numbers up. Therefore, *you* can change them too. Now where's that calculator?

Even more distressing is that introducing the words *I* and *my* into a discussion about your prices personalizes the exchange, but not in a good way. All of a sudden, those seemingly innocent words not only refer to the prices you charge, but they also contribute to the emotional toll that speaking them can have on you.

When a seller personalizes prices with the words *I* and *my*, something changes. The negative emotional charge attached to the words often transforms self-confidence into insecurity within seconds. Keep in mind the energy frequencies emitted from words and the emotions they conjure up (chapter 2, "Open Your Mind to Success"). In this situation, the words *I* and *my* turn the communication into Success-Limiting Language.

KEY WORDS *NOT TO USE* WHEN DISCUSSING FEES

"*My* fee is $_____."

"*I* charge $_____."

"*I* could do the job for $_____."

A great strategy to take the negative emotional charge out of price discussions is to depersonalize your communication by using emotionally neutral language.

Use Emotionally Neutral Language

The only time during the selling experience when it's in your best interests to take your personality out the equation is when talking about price. Replacing the words *I* and *my* with the word *the* is a perfect solution. When you say, "*The* fee is" or "*The* price is," you depersonalize the delivery. You also send the message that the fees are objective, not subjective. They're based on realities of the marketplace. In other words, *you* didn't make the prices up. It's clear that there are costs associated with the delivery of *the* products and services—all of which are factored into "*the* price."

Another terrific, emotionally neutral word to use during price discussions is the word *investment*, as in "The investment is . . ." or "Your investment is . . ." Like all solutions provided throughout this book, pick the examples that best fit your market and your personality.

Kelly's Keepers
Stay objective about prices.
"My price . . ." becomes "The price . . ."

The price conversation would now sound like this: "The first option we talked about, which meets all your needs, is priced at $X. Alternatively, if we were to meet your top needs [most pressing needs, immediate needs . . .], the second option is $Y, which is still a great value for the money [your investment]. And for $Z, there's the third option. It could provide a short-term solution [get you started]."

Silence Is Golden

After the prices are stated, silence on your part is golden. During the role-playing example, the seller cracked when Coach Kelly took a nanosecond to reflect on the prices. The seller didn't recognize that just as it's important to give customers time to think when you ask a question or to check in to confirm that you didn't miss anything, it's equally important to keep your mouth buttoned up when talking money. Give the buyer that precious time to think through what you've said.

Don't Play Guessing Games

Don't even try to guess or gauge how well the buyer is taking the news. For all you know, they could be thinking about how to justify spending even more money than previously discussed. It may not even occur to them to purchase the cheapest thing offered. So take the time to pause. Then follow up by asking, "How are these options working for you?"

If you hear anything other than "Everything's on target," use any of the Just Ask the Customer questions outlined in the chart earlier. Remember, even though you thought you'd already narrowed down the buyer's must-have list, things can change. It's your willingness to work until the best solutions are found that can result in a sale.

Ask Kelly

When the time comes to put selling solutions into a proposal, several questions come up. Listed here are the top concerns that professionals talk to me about and some of my responses.

Seller's Question: How quickly should I get a proposal to the buyer?

Kelly's Answer: Get your quote and proposals to the buyer as quickly as possible. A high level of excitement can be generated when a client feels you have a great product or solution for them. However, the window of opportunity can sometimes be slim. People are busy and move on to other things fast. This means their priorities can change. It's always best to ask, "When do you need this?"

Seller's Question: What are the best ways to present a quote?

Kelly's Answer: When your proposal is ready, here are my preferences for delivery:

1st Choice: In person

2nd Choice: By phone

3rd Choice: Via e-mail

4th Choice: Fax

5th Choice: Overnight courier

As discussed in chapter 5, "Sell without Selling," any time you are face to face with a buyer, you're in a much better position to continue to build the relationship, ask questions, and do your paraphrasing, recapping, and check-ins.

The reality is that most decision makers have little time to sit through numerous meetings. If you can't speak in person, your second-best choice is to deliver your quote over the phone. If there are several decision makers, you can hold a conference call. There are many free conference call companies that you can work with. Each caller simply pays their own long distance charges. Some services also offer you the option of purchasing a toll-free number for the call. You may also want to contact your phone provider. Many provide conference-calling features in their service plans.

The third option is to send your quote via e-mail as an attachment. Always call first to say that you'll be sending an attachment. Then tell the person that you will follow up to make sure they received the e-mail. Regrettably, people have lost contracts because their proposal was trapped in a spam blocker.

You can fax your proposal. And as a last resort you can send it via overnight courier. Keep in mind that whenever you can't speak directly to a buyer, you need to prearrange a follow-up call to find out how the buying options meet their needs.

Seller's Question: What is the ideal number of options to offer?

Kelly's Answer: A maximum of three options seem to be the magic number. Make sure to take the buyer's personality type into consideration. Using myself as an example, I fall headfirst into the action quadrant of a personality assessment. Comparing three of anything would be my limit. Too many options overwhelm personality types like mine. As action people, we want to make immediate decisions! Don't be surprised if we only compare the first two options before saying yes.

On the other hand, when selling to an analytical buyer—the person who loves to review lots of information—you need to know where to draw the line. There's never enough information for these folks. However, too many buying options can result in paralysis by analysis. At a certain point you need to say, "These are all the solutions we currently have that fit the needs you discussed. Let's now compare these solutions to your list."

Seller's Question: What if someone wants to buy right away? Do I mention the other options?

Kelly's Answer: Years ago, I witnessed this very situation. I had taken another professional with me into a sales meeting. We were teaming up our expertise. My counterpart outlined the first option to the panel of decision makers. The company president suddenly leaned forward and shouted, "That's perfect! Let's go for it." The president was an action-oriented decision maker. I was thrilled. However, my partner was completely thrown off balance and said, "But I haven't finished explaining all the options." Fortunately, he caught the look I shot him and backtracked with, "All right then. Let's get started." When the customer's ready to buy, let them buy.

Moving Forward

By working with your buyer, you both determined the best solutions. This enabled you to develop customized quotes with several buying options. However, there may be situations when a buyer has concerns or voices an objection.

In the next chapter you will find methods to easily relieve any buying hesitations. You will also discover how to let the sale unfold—without needing to close it. Get ready to **Listen to Hear Yes.**

Here's a quick recap of the main points we discussed to Lead with Your Best Solution:

Feature Your Benefits
Customers may be impressed with the features of your products and services. However, what they invest in are the benefits of what you offer.

Let the Customer Help Write the Proposal
Do not try to guess which solution(s) would be best for your buyer. Explore the options with your client. Then check in to confirm what will work.

Say Good-bye to Take-It-or-Leave-It Options
Offering only one buying solution can close the door on further discussion. It's like shouting, "Here it is! Take it or leave it." Instead, provide up to three targeted solutions for the buyer to choose from.

Give Women What They Really Want
Women shop by comparison. Give a woman several options to assess. If you don't, you just handed her an engraved invitation to check out the competition.

Look through the Eyes of a Top Decision Maker
Prepare every proposal and quotation as if it were being presented to a busy corporate decision maker.

4 Steps to a Great Written Proposal
Remind the buyer of problem(s) to be solved and desired outcomes. Provide customized options. Use proactive calls to action.

Bottom-Up Pricing Doesn't Float

Offering the most inexpensive solution first makes it difficult for a buyer to justify investing in your premium solution(s).

Use Kelly's Rule of 20s to Formulate Prices and Packages

Put together a maximum of three buying packages. Within each package, offer a differing number of options (features and benefits). Present the packages from the top (most expensive) to the bottom (least expensive).

Give Boring Face-to-Face Presentations the Heave-Ho

When providing a quotation in person, use the 4 Steps to a Great Face-to-Face Proposal and Kelly's Rule of 20s to organize your presentation.

Change Your Delivery with Women and Men

Women and men will respond differently to a seller's approach. Discuss personalized solutions with women. Talk about proven solutions with men.

Discuss Your Price—Without Throwing Up

Price discussions can feel personal. Depersonalize your delivery by eliminating the pronouns I and my. Instead use emotionally neutral language such as "The price is . . ."

Ask Kelly

Do not try to guess your way out of situations. Learn from the pros. When in doubt, ask other experts for their help, solutions, and wisdom.

8

Listen to Hear Yes

Congratulations!

Working with your buyer has enabled you to experience amazing results. However, at this point you may be wondering a few things: Is it really possible to write up the sale without hearing a single buying objection? And what about writing up the sale without asking, "So, are you ready to buy?" Can that actually happen? The answers are yes and yes!

It is absolutely possible to sell without ever hearing a single buying objection. The OutSell Yourself process was specifically designed to ease any concerns as the sale unfolds. Think about the steps you have taken. Throughout the discussion, you asked purposeful, open-ended questions to uncover real needs. You also paraphrased back key points to make sure you got everything right. Anything that wasn't clear or correct was addressed—on the spot.

Before you put together your product or service recommendations, you checked in again to make sure you were headed in the right direction. Then when you presented your customized solutions, you provided several options for your buyer to choose from.

If the proposed solutions needed to be adjusted or changed, you made it known that you'd do that—until there was an exact fit.

The same positive outcome applies to writing up the sale without having to ask, "So, are you ready to buy?" When you do a great job of uncovering real needs and demonstrate that you have what it takes to get the job done, most buyers say yes by the end of the initial conversation. Why would they talk to someone else? It's evident that you understand them and their situation and that you have the perfect solutions!

Eliminate *All* Buying Objections and Concerns

If you do find yourself in a situation where a customer voices objections or concerns, do not give yourself a hard time. Hesitancy from a buyer doesn't necessarily mean that you didn't ask the right questions, nor does it imply that you didn't check in enough during the sales process to find out where you stood.

Some concerns may be related to the customer's negative buying experiences in the past. Then there are some industries or particular situations where the same issues always crop up. And sometimes a customer simply gets cold feet when it comes time to sign a contract or pull out a credit card.

Whatever the circumstance, it's essential that you let the buyer express any uncertainty. You need to know what is going on. How else can you resolve whatever could be holding them back from saying yes?

Here's the interesting thing. When you respond to objections, you actually keep the sales conversation moving. So consider objections as a big window into the customer's mind. They reveal what a person is really thinking. Instead of dreading or avoiding objections, welcome them. Then deal with them head on.

Act Like a Girl Guide and Girl Scout

While I was growing up in Canada, the Girl Guides taught me to always be prepared. I took the message to heart. Before speaking with a client, I make it a point to put myself in their shoes. It then becomes very easy to consider any potential concerns. It also becomes easy to prepare my responses in advance.

To build confidence in your ability to handle any objections, you can also anticipate them. I'm not talking about freaking out beforehand. I'm talking about considering what you might hear. Then you too can practice your proactive responses and be Girl Guide and Girl Scout ready.

> *We are what we repeatedly do.*
> *Excellence, therefore, is not an act but a habit.*
> ARISTOTLE

When you respond to your customer, turn and run away from any of the "Worst Ways to Respond to an Objection" listed below.

WORST WAYS TO RESPOND TO AN OBJECTION

1. Defend your position:
   "I don't know why you need to talk to other suppliers. Our company has won 27 awards. Obviously we do great work. Here, look at our brochure one more time."

2. Argue with the customer:
   "What do you mean it won't work? Our solution is a great solution. I'll tell you 99 more reasons why."

3. Respond without uncovering the real issue:
   "We're too expensive? We have the lowest rates around. Let me go over this again."

Wow—those were horrible responses. Regrettably, they are very true to life. As a matter of fact, they were adapted from "techniques" that people have used during role-plays in some of my training sessions. Ouch. We will consider them the before photos. I promise that the after shots will turn out much better. You'll find everything in focus, and everyone will end up looking good.

Delve Deeper and Reengage the Customer

To resist slipping into defending, arguing, or neglecting to respond to the real problem, ask questions to delve deeper to uncover the *real issues*. This will also return the customer to the Discovery Dialogue. During this process, as mentioned in chapter 2, "Open Your Mind to Success," like energy attracts like energy. It's important to remain relaxed and optimistic. Make sure not to mirror any anxiety or wavering expressed by the buyer. Do not imitate their uncertainty. Lead with the positive energy that you would like to see in the exchange.

> *Everything that irritates us about others*
> *can lead us to an understanding of ourselves.*
> CARL JUNG, PSYCHIATRIST

Quit Doing Back Flips for Pennies

The most common objections that sellers ask for help with are related to price and budgets. Because money issues can be a hot-button topic for buyers and sellers, we'll use price concerns as an example of how to best respond to objections. You'll soon see how to probe and reply in a nonconfrontational way. Once you see the model in action, ideas should surface about how to apply the principles to other types of buying concerns. Remember, these are only guidelines. Like all the skills we've covered, adjust everything to fit you and your situation.

Surprise!

Even though you asked for and got the buyer's approximate price range or budget, price objections can still pop up when you present your sales solutions. A buyer could surprise you with "That seems very expensive." You might say to yourself, "What's going on? They told me what they wanted to spend, and we are within budget." Well, it could be that the customer expected to get more for the money. But at this point, you don't know that for certain.

Rather than panic and discount your prices, it is best not to make any assumptions. Instead, you need to ask questions and delve deeper. The following true-to-life sales scenario shows you how the process works. My comments demonstrate the types of real issues that could be uncovered.

Scenario: "That seems very expensive."

It's not uncommon for buyers to be out of touch with what products and services really cost. This is especially true when the commodity is new to the customer or if it has been a long time since they've purchased something similar. In either case, resist panicking and immediately slashing your prices. As discussed in chapter 7, "Lead with Your Best Solution," you may simply have to educate the client on what something similar costs today.

Do your check-in:

"So that I understand, the service seems expensive compared to what?"

Customer response:

"Compared to the last time I bought this kind of service."

Do a further check-in:

"When was that?"

Customer response:

"Five years ago."

Reassure and educate:

"No wonder it seems expensive. I had the same reaction when I bought my latest car. Like everything, prices have gone up. Here's what the industry rates are today and what you typically get . . ."

As demonstrated, when you probe to find out what's really behind the question, things become clearer. The real issues come to light. Then you can decide how best to respond. Listed below are other common price objections and concerns, along with responses you can use.

Kelly's Keepers
Price often becomes an issue
when it isn't clear why something is worth the money.

It Really Does Seem Too Expensive

As the sale is about to wrap up, some buyers consider challenging the price to be part of the process. This can occur even after telling you how much they "love everything." As frustrating as the situation may seem, it's best to go in the direction that the horse is heading. Saddle up—we're off.

COMMON PRICE OBJECTIONS & CONCERNS
WITH YOUR RESPONSES

"It's too expensive."

"Just to be certain that this is a direct comparison—it's expensive compared to what?"

"The competition is cheaper."

"To make sure that the same services [product, option, levels of expertise, deliverables . . .] are being offered, please help me to understand what you're comparing with. What is the competition offering?"

If the direct competition actually is cheaper, you can say, "I guess the decision will have to be based on which supplier [company, person] you feel best understands your situation [needs, expectations] and will provide the service you want. What questions do we still need to address?"

"Things have changed. The price is higher than our current budget."

"Well, let's look at what can be eliminated or adjusted to meet your budget. What is a must-have option for you?"

"That seems expensive."

The following response was developed for a client providing customer service training to call centers: "It can seem expensive if the return on investment isn't taken into consideration: If you don't mind me asking, approximately how much money would be saved in hourly wages if the average customer complaint was resolved in one to two calls instead of the current four to six?" You can easily adapt the ROI example: "How many units would you have to sell to recoup your investment?"

The following response was developed for a client who sells high-end consumer products: "Our customers find that they actually save money in the end because they don't need to replace the products as often. How long would you like the product [service, solution] to last?"

As you have seen, each response followed a similar pattern. The issue was addressed and a question was asked to reengage the sales conversation. Now we have another scenario to consider: working with the buyer who's reluctant to ever reveal their budget.

A Budget Appears out of Nowhere

During the sales process, you could meet up with a buyer who won't give you an approximate budget under any circumstances. Some customers have been oversold in the past, and they don't want a repeat performance. Their strategy becomes, "I'll put the budget under lock and key, then wait to see how close the price is to what I'm willing to pay."

Others hide the numbers in hopes that you will provide a price lower than they would normally spend. Whatever the reason, it's best to be prepared for these situations too. The following examples will help. Don't get off that horse yet.

OBJECTIONS FROM BUYERS WHO WON'T REVEAL THEIR BUDGET WITH YOUR RESPONSES

"I don't want to spend too much!"
> "Great. Now there is a budget to work with! So what price range were you thinking of spending?"

"Your fee [price] is too high."
> "Well, that depends on what you're trying to accomplish. Given what we have discussed, it can be a great ROI [value for your money]. We should talk about the budget you now have to work with and identify the most critical issues that we must deal with. So what price range are you looking to spend?"

"Is this your best price?"
> "Yes, it certainly is. We always quote our best price. This way we don't waste your time or ours. What price range would you like to work with?"

In these scenarios, rather than defend the price, the seller acknowledged that there was now a budget to work with. In two of the examples, the seller showed the customer the benefits to them of sharing the approximate budget. In all examples, there was a reengage question. The purpose of the question was to finally find out the approximate budget—information many buyers will finally reveal. With that cleared up, there's another situation we need to cover: how to respond to the statement, "We really like your stuff [products, services, ideas, solutions], but ..."

> *Some days you feel like you're the dog*
> *and other days like you're the hydrant.*
> UNKNOWN

We Really Like Your Stuff ... But

When you hear, "We really like your stuff *but* ... ," several things could be going on. For one, the buyer's situation could have changed. They may not be in a position to buy at this time. If that's the case, it is best to respect their decision, while keeping the door open. The upcoming section, "Let Go of Stalker Style Follow-Ups," shows you how to stay in contact with potential buyers—without being pushy.

On the other hand, it could be that the customer's wish list was bigger than their bank account. Typically, the sentence would finish with "Could you drop the price a bit? We're on a tight budget." Here are some responses to choose from.

Your first response option: "It's important that I maintain fee integrity by keeping fees consistent with all my customers. I'm sure you understand." This subtle yet effective statement delivers the message that the fee is the fee—no discounts. Clients generally respond in one of two ways.

Customer's first possible response: "Oh, of course I understand." This indicates to both of you that the conversation about price-cutting has run its course. More often than not, an agreement is then written up at full price. At least that has been my experience.

Customer's second possible response: "I understand. But $X is all we have to spend. However, you'll probably get more business [sales, referrals] from this." Caution! Red alert! When people say that dropping the price could lead to more business, it's often not high-paying work, which is implied. What typically ends up happening is that you do a lot of work for low money, for that client only.

Several customers with truly tight budgets have crossed my path over the years. If you really want to work with the client, you can counter with any of the following options.

Request a Referral: "To make up the balance of the fee, I would offset it against my promotion budget. This means I would ask for a testimonial letter and introductions to companies/individuals who could benefit from my service/product."

Trade-offs: You can trade off any fee reduction for products/services of equal value from the client.

Give a Referral: "I understand that your budget is limited. Let me refer you to people [companies, businesses] with products/services/expertise in that price range."

Do a Final Check-In

If you sense that the buyer may have concerns or objections that haven't been voiced, you can ask, "If you don't mind me asking, what needs to happen [what concerns do you need addressed, what questions do you want answered] for you to be assured that this would be the right buying decision?" Wait patiently for the response. Respond openly and honestly to whatever comes up.

It's Your Turn

It's your turn to consider what types of buying concerns you might hear. As mentioned earlier, to make it easy, put yourself in your buyer's shoes. Then imagine any possible objections or concerns you may have to buying your goods. Write everything down. Using the previous examples as a model, record your responses.

COMMON OBJECTIONS & CONCERNS

Your Delve Deeper Responses

1.

2.

3.

4.

5.

Don't Give Up–Give Back

There's one more scenario you may have to address. If you sell within the not-for-profit sector, there are some groups and organizations that may have little or no budget. Years ago, I created my **Give Back to the Community** policy to deal with the numerous requests for reduced fees and freebies. Each year up to three organizations can benefit from my Give Back to the Community rates, which are lower than regular rates. Setting a limit on how many organizations will benefit each year ensures that the **Keep Kelly McCormick Afloat** fund remains solvent. Others have found that using my Give Back to the Community policy has kept them afloat too.

The bottom line: Whenever you respond to any type of objection or concern, the key is to let the buyer voice their thoughts. Then you can delve deeper to uncover the real issues and arrive at a mutually satisfying resolution. Remember, you can do this at any point during the OutSell Yourself process.

Stand Back as the Customer Asks to Buy

You are now ready to write up the sale. The OutSell Yourself process served as an interactive map. Every question you asked revealed more and more of the details until the perfect solution became apparent to you and the customer. Any buying concerns or objections were handled with care. Now the perfect solution is staring both of you in the face. It's an obvious choice. You and your products and services are the right answer. You did a terrific job, so don't choke now and try to pull a rabbit out of your hat.

The Hard-Sell Close

There are sellers who turn into magicians when it comes time to ring up a sale. They'll use almost any closing trick to get the customer to say, "Yes, I'll buy"—even when they don't need to. The most common fear-based maneuver is often referred to as the hard-sell close. Most of us have had the regrettable experience of being on the receiving end of this tactic. It's when the seller exploits a weakness or need that the buyer trustingly disclosed. Without pausing to take a breath, they pile on a high-pressure call to action: "You told me that immediate delivery [follow-up service, training, product style, results . . .] would be most important to you. But let's face it: Your situation won't improve on its own. So what are you prepared to do about it?"

Then there's the softer version of the hard sell—if that's possible: "I've just told you about all the benefits of our service, which are exactly what you said you wanted to solve the problem of low productivity [morale, turnover]. So what's stopping you from making a decision on this right now?"

Had enough? There's one more soft-hard sell close that is equally direct and to the point—not to mention deceptive: "I don't know how long I can hold these prices [rates, fees] for you."

The Final Push

Giving a final push to close a sale can be risky. It can also grind to a screaming halt all that great work you did to be upfront and honorable. When a seller pushes to close the sale, the buyer often hits the brakes and looks for an emergency exit.

Customers aren't the only ones who dislike the traditional closing process. After years of hearing the confessions of professionals who admitted that closing the sale caused them unbelievable distress, I've come to the conclusion that asking for a sale puts people in the most vulnerable position imaginable: They could be rejected.

Stop the Madness!!!

The solution? Don't ask for the sale. Let me be clear. *Do not* under any circumstances mumble any of the following: "Should I write up a contract?" "Are you ready to move forward on this deal?" and the biggest mouthful of them all, "Do you want to hire me?"

Nope—don't do any of this. And also do away with providing a price or proposal and then uttering a weak call to action: "I'll call you in a few days and check in to see how everything met your needs." (Then, when I don't hear from you, I'll send seventeen e-mails and leave daily voice-mail messages for three weeks.) The in-person version of this is, "Well think it over and get back to me." Handing over the controls or pushing to close a sale rarely works.

Let the Sale Unfold

Every step you have taken with the client has been in partnership. The sale has been unfolding throughout the process. At this point, it can be easier and more comfortable for a buyer to make several small buying decisions. Breaking the decision into smaller pieces eliminates a lot of anxiety for both of you.

You'll now see a variety of sale-unfolding statements. Each varies in the level of commitment that the customer makes. Obviously, you wouldn't use all of the statements. Apply the one(s) that fit best.

SALE-UNFOLDING STATEMENTS

"When you review the options, which do you prefer—A, B, or C?"

"The next step is to get your signature on this agreement and a deposit, and then I'll order the product and have it delivered to you by next Thursday." You can also begin this conversation by asking, "So what do you think about what we've discussed so far?" If you hear, "Sounds good," then you introduce the next steps. If you hear an objection or concerns, address them. Check in again: "Anything else we need to cover in order for you to feel good about making this decision?"

"If you like what you've seen [what we've discussed], why not give it a try? We can get started tomorrow, or is there a better day for you?"

"Now that you're aware of the benefits of our solution [what we can accomplish], when would you like delivery [to get started]?"

"We have identified [found, narrowed down] some great benefits [solutions, products, services] to meet your needs. How would you like to proceed?"

"I can hold the date [hold the product, reserve space] for you while you check on the best timing [financing]. What date(s) did you have in mind?"

"When we begin to service your account, would you like me to introduce it to your people [staff, associates, sales team, family]?"

"I can do this work for you now [next week, on the date asked]. I just need [a deposit, your authorization, your signature here]."

"Would you want this shipped [this delivered to your home or office, immediate delivery, to take it now, to include additional options, to pay by credit card or check]?"

There are many small decision-making points you can offer. Buyers appreciate this approach. Whenever they can breeze through the details, it is much easier to purchase anything from a car to a condo. However, there are some situations where they might need to talk to others or sleep on it before making a final decision.

Kelly's Keepers
Present small decision-making points
to make it easy for customers to say yes.

Let Me Think It Over

Some decisions may require further thought. Sometimes associates, family members, or others have to be consulted. Offer to help: "I'd be pleased to have a meeting [conversation] with you and your boss [neighbor, friend, cat, gardener, psychic] to fill them in on what we've discussed and answer any questions. When is a good time for all of us to meet?"

Some customers will take you up on it. When you're there to explain things, it can keep them out of the hot seat. Let's face it: Who wants to risk screwing up when describing the solutions or to be made to feel they have to justify why certain decisions were made? Not me. I'd let you "talk to my people."

If you hear, "I need to think about it," you can say, "I understand. What information can I provide or questions can I answer to help you with your decision-making process?" For all you know, they could be considering a very minor point. Opening the door to further discussion could eliminate any concerns within minutes.

Gain the Agreement to Follow Up

For the buyer who hasn't already said yes to your solution, the best course of action would be to set a date and time to follow up. This will stop you from being *that* seller. The one who says, "I'll call you in a few days and check in to see how the proposal met your needs." (Then, when I don't hear from you, I'll stalk you to the ends of the earth.)

182

You gain permission to follow up by stating the purpose of the call: "I realize that you're busy. When would it be best to follow up to answer questions, make any changes to the proposal, and talk about our next steps?"

Confirm that you will initiate the call. Then recap the purpose of the call: "So I will call you next Tuesday at 8:30 a.m. to answer questions, make any changes to the proposal, and discuss our next steps."

By the way, scheduling any type of meetings, appointments, or follow-up calls for "next week" increases the likelihood that it will actually happen. I've discovered that for some unknown reason, psychologically, no one has time this week. But everyone has time "next week."

Kelly's Keepers
People are often "too busy this week."
Book follow-ups for "next week."

Let Go of Stalker-Style Follow-Ups

Whoops, the customer missed the follow-up appointment. Luckily, you got on it right away. You called and e-mailed twice a day, morning and night, for five weeks in a row. But nothing happened. Well, that may not be true. Several things could have happened. But most of us go straight to "I knew it. They weren't going to hire me [buy from me]!"

Reasons Why Buyers Go Missing

If a company or individual didn't buy immediately, missed a scheduled follow-up, or didn't respond to your messages, it could be for many reasons, including:

- They died. (Unless you're in the funeral business, this probably isn't good news. Check in later to find out who is now looking after things.)
- Someone else died. (Send a card.)
- They had a deadline of their own. (Call and say, "I understand. Given the current situation, when would you like me to contact you?")
- Their company changed direction. (Someone in the team/family might have come up with a new plan. Ask, "What's the new direction, and how can I help [contribute to your success, make things easier for you . . .]?")
- Their priorities changed. (They needed to spend the money somewhere else, like on the mortgage. Ask, "What's your current plan [situation]?" because there may be an opportunity to provide a smaller-scale buying solution.)
- They hired a different vendor for "political" reasons: "I'll hire your company and then you can hire us." (Keep the door open by saying, "I understand. And in case that vendor [company, supplier, person] can't meet all your needs, I will keep in touch.")
- There were internal position changes and the decision maker has changed. (Call to introduce yourself and find out where things stand.)
- The economy took a downturn, and the budget was pulled. (That sucks. Check in later, as the problem to be solved probably didn't disappear.)
- The breadwinner lost their job. (Give them time to regroup.)

Love Me—Hate Me—Just Don't Ignore Me

Yes, it would have been very nice if the buyer had called to tell you that things had changed. You're right; it wasn't considerate to leave things so unfinished.

But here's the thing: Most people don't know how to deliver bad news. Think of all those heartbroken people waiting by phones after first dates. So the question becomes: Do you call them? Would it be better for you to sit and wait, and wait, and wait for them to call you? Well, if you haven't heard from a date, the answer is no, move on. If it is a buyer who didn't call back, the answer is yes, contact them. But don't chase them like a stalker.

> *How people treat you is their Karma.*
> *How you respond is yours.*
> WAYNE DYER

Worst Follow-Up Statements

The worst follow-up statement has the word *you* in it: "I'm just calling you because I haven't heard back from you."

Inserting the word *you* into a follow-up inquiry suddenly turns an innocent check-in into a personal remark. In this situation, a person could feel that their behavior is being judged. Yes, the customer knows they haven't returned your calls or e-mails. However, when they hear "I'm just calling you because I haven't heard back from you," they could also perceive that they're being made to feel guilty or, even worse, are being nagged. Of course that's not the intention of the exchange. However, when people feel hounded and the exchange becomes overly personal, they quickly lose enthusiasm for hiring the chaser.

Here's the final equally abysmal follow-up statement: "I'm just calling to touch base." That line has been so overused that people don't even hear it any more. Enough said about that.

Best Follow-Up Statements

The best follow-up happens when the seller takes responsibility for making the call and provides clear follow-through options for the decision maker. For example, if the customer misses the scheduled follow-up call, here is your plan B.

If you don't hear back, create a logical reason to contact the decision maker: "Hi, sorry we weren't able to connect last week. Obviously, it's been busy for both of us. [You were busy. Busy wondering why they didn't call.] If you can let me know the best time to talk this week or next, then I will set aside the time for you."

You may not get an immediate response. So the question becomes how many messages should you leave? I suggest one to two more, spaced out over a month. And here's another important tip: When leaving a voice-mail message, don't treat your communication as a live performance. People tend to ramble when leaving messages. Think of how you respond when listening to long-winded speeches. How often have you hit delete or fast forward in the middle of such a message? My point? Get to the point.

Kelly's Keepers

In a great voice-mail message, you make your point
by getting to the point.

If you still don't hear back, then make a final call. This call is the closure call: "It's never my intention to bother anyone with repeated calls. So I thought we could put some closure on this. If my proposal wasn't the right fit for whatever reason, or if you decided to go with another vendor, it's okay to let me know. I can handle it. Please feel free to call or e-mail, and I'll know not to keep calling about this proposal. Thanks in advance for your feedback."

Depending on the situation or the person, you may not get an immediate response to your closure call. If that's the case I suggest you give them some space. Now here is a big shocker: You may still hear from them later, even much later. This has happened to me and to others many, many times. Refer to the section above entitled "Reasons Why Buyers Go Missing" to remind yourself that things come up for companies and individuals. Silence doesn't always mean no. It sometimes means just not right now. Keep the faith!

Whenever in doubt about what to say or how often to follow up, think about how you like to be treated as a customer. In seconds, you'll have your answer.

Stay in the Loop

When you don't hear back from the client right away and you are giving them space, you can still do things to keep yourself in the loop. Try some passive marketing. Periodically send cards, articles, information, and business announcements. Here is another surprise: You may not have been the right fit for this customer; however, they could refer you to someone else. Better yet, as previously mentioned, they could call in the future when you least expect it! For now, give thanks for all those who did say yes!

Wrap Up the Sale with a Bow

Hearing yes can be the sweetest sound. You are about to write up the sale. However, whether your buyer said yes on the spot or some time later, you have a final step to take. I'm talking about doing a Wrap-Up-the-Sale-with-a-Bow check-in.

Signed, Sealed, Delivered

You can only deliver as promised when you have confirmed *all* the details. Even if you think that everything was crystal clear, be forewarned: Memories can become fuzzy. This often happens when the selling process was lengthy, involved several people, or required a number of passes to find the perfect solution. Customers can forget important points . . . until something hasn't been delivered.

Another costly disaster occurs when minor assumptions have been made by either the seller or buyer. Unfortunately, these situations can crop up regardless of how much information you gather in advance. So do a final check-in.

What-When-Where-Price-How

The Wrap-Up-the-Sale-with-a-Bow check-in method requires you to ask questions that cover *what, when, where, price,* and *how.* Whether you are selling a product or a service, you need to confirm the buyer's contact information, what they are to receive, by when, the delivery terms, final price, and how payment will be invoiced and paid. Once you have verified the details, make sure to put *everything* in writing. Then share it with the buyer. This way there will be no surprises awaiting anyone after the sale. You will both feel the confidence of knowing that your solutions are a perfect fit and that you can and will deliver as promised.

Moving Forward

Throughout the OutSell Yourself process, you asked purposeful questions which enabled you and the buyer to find the perfect solution at the right price. If the buyer had any objections and concerns, you listened well and then responded openly and pro-actively. Instead of trying to close the sale, you offered a variety of small choices to decide on. This enabled the sale to unfold without pressure.

If the buyer didn't say yes immediately, you didn't fall prey to any stalker-style follow-up techniques. Instead, you gained your buyer's agreement to let you check in at a later date.

Once you got the green light to write up the sale, you did a final check-in. You wrapped everything up by asking pertinent questions to make sure that you would indeed deliver as promised—which you will! Even better, this now puts you in the perfect position to build on your success. So read the final chapter and find out how to get even **More Sales, More Often, with Less Effort.**

LISTEN TO HEAR YES—RECAP

Here's a quick recap of the main points we discussed to
Listen to Hear Yes:

Eliminate *All* Buying Objections and Concerns
When you respond to any objections or concerns, do not
defend, argue, or neglect to address the real problem. Ask
questions to delve deeper, uncover the real issues, and reengage the customer back into the sales process.

Quit Doing Back Flips for Pennies
The most common objections sellers ask for help with are
related to price and budgets, as money issues can be a
hot-button topic. The same model of how to reply in a nonconfrontational way can be applied to other types of buying
concerns.

Don't Give Up—Give Back
If you sell within the not-for-profit sector, some groups and
organizations may have little or no budget. Use my Give Back
to the Community policy. Up to three organizations a year can
benefit from rates which are lower than regular fees.

Stand Back as the Customer Asks to Buy
Do not try to close the sale. You let the sale unfold when you
eliminate buying pressure and offer a series of small points
for decisions to be made on.

Let Go of Stalker-Style Follow-Ups
If the discussion does not result in an immediate sale, you
gain agreement to follow up when you state the purpose(s)
for any future contact and set a firm date and time to speak.

Wrap Up the Sale with a Bow

You can only deliver as promised when you have confirmed all the details and put them in writing. The Wrap-Up-the-Sale-with-a-Bow check-in method covers what, when, where, price, and how.

9

More Sales, More Often, with Less Effort

As the work rolled in, I made yet another earth-shattering discovery. You can continue to build on your success long after delivery of your product or services. However, simply waving good-bye to your customer can cost you a fortune in future income.

Sellers who know how to take customer relationships to the next level can tap into a wealth of business. And I am about to show you how to do this. Like everything else covered in this book, the next steps you take to increase your sales are easy to implement. They also keep your database active and growing.

Apply Kelly's Potent Three-Part After-Sale Inquiry

After the sale, you can do something so powerful that it will exceed your buyer's expectations. It's something that few professionals bother with: You can call to *check in*. This is especially important after you've sold to a woman, because women don't just invest in product and service solutions—they invest in you too. You may think you only sold a commodity or service, but in her eyes you just became part of her team. If she has any problems, your number's now programmed into her cell or company phone. The women I've interviewed say they expect you to provide service and aftercare. Men too say they are impressed with sellers who will go the extra mile. So don't stop now. It's your time to shine.

Kelly's Keepers
The after-sale check-in often uncovers
more selling opportunities.

Pick Your Moment to Shine

The timing of your follow-up call depends on what you sold and how long it will take the customer to use and evaluate your solution. For example, if you sold a vacuum cleaner, you could call within two weeks of the purchase. By then the appliance should have been used at least once, you would hope. After delivery of complex equipment or services such as consulting, the check-in time would be longer. You might contact your client anywhere from one to six months after the completion of your project.

Call—Don't E-mail

When you do follow up, it's best to call the client. Keep in mind that any time you find an opportunity to speak directly, it strengthens your relationship. But before you dial, preframe your conversation with my **Three-Part Inquiry** process. This avoids potentially destructive rambling on your part. Then when you make your focused call, in addition to blowing your buyer's mind, the conversation will often open the door to the next sale.

Begin with "I am calling to see how everything [the product, the service] is working for you and to find out *what questions, comments, or concerns you* might have."

Your inquiry works for many reasons. It allows the customer to give feedback which can be excellent to know. Plus it provides a forum for them to voice any concerns. It's better for you to hear about problems directly. You can then address them on the spot. And the best part is that your customer gets to plan out loud and discuss their other needs. The next selling opportunities are revealed. Remember to ask for referrals and a testimonial.

Kelly's Keepers

Be one of the few sellers who will ask
for a testimonial and referrals.

Uncover Hidden Selling Opportunities with Referrals

If you sold your solution to a midsized to large company, corporation, or association, you are likely sitting on a mountain of new business. You can uncover gems of hidden selling opportunities by asking, "What other departments [organizations, branches, franchises, industries] do you feel could benefit from this product/service?" When you receive the information, add, "Whom should I speak with, and can I use your name as a reference?"

Another selling opportunity appears with this question: "Which of your suppliers do you feel could improve their service to you if they had a similar solution?" Again, follow up with "Whom should I speak with, and can I use your name as a reference?"

You can ask for referrals from individuals too. When a person compliments you on what you sold or mentions the great results they've had, you can say, "Thank you. And the best compliment you could give me would be to pass my name on to others." (My dentist taught me that. And it works! I've referred others to him.)

Use Testimonials to Get More Business

Using testimonials can also increase your business dramatically. The easiest method I know of to collect feedback is one recommended several times throughout the book: *Just ask*. As straightforward as the technique seems, many professionals don't know how or when to do that. Well, that ends right now.

> *Our greatest weakness lies in giving up.*
> *The most certain way to succeed is always to try one more time.*
> THOMAS EDISON, INVENTOR

The Ask Technique

Similar to asking for a referral, the perfect time to ask for a testimonial is when the buyer has expressed appreciation for your product, service, or customer service.

When working with a company or association, you may find that most decision makers are too busy to write a testimonial themselves. If that's the case, then offer to write it yourself. And make it powerful. It quickly becomes your next selling tool. But be sure to send it to the person for their input and final approval.

When selling to individuals, you can say, "I'm glad we met your needs. I'd really appreciate sharing your feedback with other customers. May I quote you?" Most people will say yes. Especially if you do a terrific job serving a woman, she often says yes without hesitation. Women tend to be very open about passing on helpful information.

Elements of a Powerful Testimonial

A powerful testimonial speaks to several elements. It provides positive feedback on the product or service solution and how you demonstrated your professionalism [expertise, knowledge, attention to detail, willingness to go the extra mile, ability to identify and solve complex problems, eagerness to source hard-to-find solutions].

It includes a name and/or position and a company name. Informal surveys I've conducted with entrepreneurs and business owners reveal that most don't believe the authenticity of a testimonial if it doesn't identify the source. In other words, without a person's name, position, or company name, many people think you simply made it up.

Connect with Buyers through the Wired World

The wired world provides ample opportunity to connect with buyers and collect even more positive feedback—that is, if you make it easy. People don't have time to waste navigating any form of technology that isn't intuitive. Your website can include a "Tell Us What You Think" link. Make sure to have a "Contact Us" link or e-mail address that stands out. How about programming your blog to be an interactive forum? Why not provide a 1-800 number to call you? Your e-mail signature can also provide a variety of social networking links, such as Twitter, LinkedIn, and Facebook. The sky is the limit on how innovative you can be when communicating with satisfied buyers.

Be creative. Use unconventional thinking.
And have the guts to carry it out.
LEE IACOCCA, AUTOMOBILE EXECUTIVE AND AUTHOR

Let Your Satisfied Customers Sell for You

As soon as you get the testimonials and feedback, start using them. Insert your customers' comments into everything from your sales conversations to your promotional materials. When selling to women, highlighting testimonials from other women can be a brilliant marketing initiative. A woman's endorsement becomes an influential sales tool. Women trust each other to tell it like it is. Men also value hearing positive endorsements. So let every one of your satisfied customers sell for you.

Your customers can keep you busy for years!

MORE SALES, MORE OFTEN, WITH LESS EFFORT—RECAP

Here's a quick recap of the main points we discussed to get More Sales, More Often, with Less Effort:

Apply Kelly's Potent Three-Part After-Sale Inquiry

After the sale make a follow-up call. Avoid potentially destructive ramblings on your part with my Three-Part Inquiry process. It can uncover additional selling opportunities.

Uncover Hidden Selling Opportunities with Referrals

If you sold your solution to a midsized to large company, corporation, or association, there can be many great opportunities to ask for internal referrals to other departments and even to the suppliers of your customers and clients. When selling to individuals, you can ask for referrals within their inner circle.

Use Testimonials to Get More Business

The perfect time to ask for a testimonial is when the buyer has expressed appreciation for your product, service, or customer service. A powerful testimonial speaks to several elements, including the effectiveness of your product or service solution and how you demonstrated your professionalism.

Connect with Buyers through the Wired World

The wired world provides ample opportunity to collect positive feedback through blogs, Twitter, LinkedIn, and Facebook, a 1-800 number, and more. But you must make it easy for clients to find you and to communicate with you. People are busy. They don't have time to waste navigating any form of technology that isn't intuitive.

Let Your Satisfied Customers Sell for You

Insert your satisfied customers' comments into everything from your sales conversations to your promotional materials. Let every one of your satisfied customers sell for you. They can keep you busy for years!

Acknowledgments

Writing this book has been an act of extreme faith and courage. During a three-year, on-again off-again, and then full-tilt pedal-to-the-metal time span, a lot happened. It took a "no matter what" attitude to keep going.

Having moved from Canada to the United States, my plate was already full. In between traveling to speak and writing my online column for *Sales and Marketing Management* magazine, I was also filling out reams of Green Card paperwork. So why not include "write a book" on the to-do list? Made perfect sense!

To add a little more drama to the adventure, I moved five times. In the middle of packing and unpacking, I also realized a dream. Holed up in Malibu, California, I got to "write a book by the ocean." What I hadn't seen in my vision was smoke. On two different occasions, fires whipped outside my seaside retreat. Both times, after sticking a finger into the acrid air and saying a huge prayer, I decided to stay put. Having lost contact with the outside world, I hunkered down and wrote.

Fortunately the smoke cleared . . . just in time for the economy to crash. However, there is an upside to writing a sales book during a bout of double-digit inflation. It gives you more credibility. Having survived, and thrived, throughout all of this, my first shout-out goes to . . . drum roll please . . . my Higher Power.

I have been kept safe and remained in the flow, no matter what. Gracias, gracias, gracias.

The next pat on the back goes to me. Yes, I am saying thanks to myself. Who knew that I would have enough staying power to write nine book drafts with endless tweaks, refinements, and rewrites? Granted, the first two drafts were a little drafty. But still, I surpassed my own iffy expectations. I wrote as I flew on planes. I wrote as I traveled in cars—while other people drove, of course. I wrote in coffee shops and at the hairdresser's. If a location could or would accommodate my moments of inspiration, I got down to business. This might explain why my laptop blew out three hard drives. (Thanks to all the computer wizards who kept rebuilding and rebooting my virtual brain.)

The next *big* show of appreciation goes to my family. My mother, Frances McCormick, has been a terrific cheerleader, motivator, and unofficial business consultant since forever. Mom, I am so grateful to you for your unwavering love and support. To my Dad, Bob McCormick, where do I begin? You have stood by me time and time again. You've also whispered sage advice, into my sometimes-blocked ears, while I've bungee-jumped through life. What a testament to love! Mom and Dad, you are both rock solid!

To my sister Cassandra LeMay, I am indebted to you for all of your free executive admin support. For over two decades, you have unraveled my latest emergency, regardless of what time zone I was in. Without your magic touch, I would still be trying to format charts, locate lost fonts, and get bullet points to line up (#&*?@#). Not to mention sorting out other endless administrative details schmetails. How do you do it? Cassie, you are a blessing, and a really smart cookie! And let's not forget my brother-in-law Darwin. During my last trip home to Toronto, you stayed up all night to reinstall my computer's entire software system (hard drive number three). Darwin, that was definitely above and beyond the call of duty!

They say that it takes a village to raise a child. Well, after this experience I would add, "It also takes a village to write a book." There are so many honorable mentions to make in this category that I'll start at the beginning of the journey. Darwin, do you remember sitting at that outdoor café on Bloor Street West in Toronto with Cassie and me? It was the night that I announced, "I am going to write a book on selling!" Chewing on some ice, you innocently said, "Don't write a straight-up business book. Make it interesting." That was music to my ears. As you work for a large institution, I felt as if I'd just received the corporate seal of approval. The last thing I wanted to do was to write a boring business book. Your endorsement set me free!

After I allowed myself to write with reckless abandonment, a fellow speaker and writer showed up to rescue my book from me! During a coffee break at the monthly Los Angeles chapter meeting of NSA (National Speakers Association), I naively turned to colleague Bob Walker and asked, "Do you know of a good content editor for my book?" The next thing I knew, e-mail addresses had been exchanged and you had agreed to look at the first draft. Bob, after reading my manuscript, you were most kind when you called to say, "Kelly, I need to teach you the rules of writing a book. Then you'll know when you've broken them." But you didn't quit there. For the next two years you checked in to cheer me on: "Keep going. Ninety percent of writers never complete their book. You will!" When I finally made it to the finish line, you took the time to review the entire manuscript—once again. Bob, your expertise, guidance, and support have been invaluable. And I love the irony that the author of *Sink or Swim Problem Solving* saved my book from drowning in excessive verbiage.

Members of CAPS (Canadian Association of Professional Speakers) also put their two cents' worth into this project. A special thanks goes to Warren Evans, CSP, Hall of Fame Professional Speaker, and Business Trends expert. I appreciated the time spent at your kitchen table as we developed "Kelly's Rule of 20s." Have you learned to cook yet?

Other experts crossed my writing path. Certified NLP Master Practitioner Linda Romano deciphered some complex information on how people access information. Linda, your input made things crystal clear. Cherie, it was brilliant of you to tell me, "Money does grow on trees. It's paper." Merci, Jocelyn Boily, for the thumbs-up on my English-to-French translation. Janice Smith, author of *Era of the Rebel: Embracing Your Individuality,* you actually volunteered to read my manuscript and give feedback. Wow. And I especially liked the message you typed on the last page, in forty-point orange font: "Good work, Kelly. Well done!"

Mary Jo Tate, you are an amazing editor. You took the time to interview me to find out what my expectations were. You made it very easy for me to sell myself on why I should hire you! Then two minutes into our working relationship, I also discovered that you were a master at paying attention to the details. Mary Jo, you're more than a professional comma pusher. You gave excellent feedback and provided ideas and suggestions that were bang on. Thanks for everything!

Spot checkers aren't just for sports. Diana Bernas you were a true blue friend. Without hesitating, you said yes to a final proofread of the book!

Graham Van Dixhorn, from Write to Your Market™, you are another of the amazing experts who gave 110% to this project. I so appreciate your diligence in working with me to put together book cover copy that captured the true essence of what OutSell Yourself is about.

During this process, I learned many lessons. Here's one: Writing a book is one thing. Getting it to print is a whole other ball game. Hobie Hobart of Dunn+Associates, you were a human filing cabinet of resources. Such expert guidance shaved years off of my book-to-print learning curve.

To my friends, family, and colleagues scattered around the globe, your support and encouragement mean more than you'll ever know. You all get equal billing, so to keep it simple, I've listed your names in alphabetical order (if I didn't screw it up). Thank you, Angela Shelton, Alana Lea, Caroline Farah, David Barcelona a.k.a. Right-Hand Man, Eileen Kwan, Elizabeth and Pumpkin Lambaer, Geoff Taylor, the "Girls from Franklin Avenue," Johnny Cole, Judith Onley, Kathy Wilson, Kim Lovisek, Lora Canary, Mark Streeter, Matthew McCormick, Max Cole, Michele Gervais, Nick Dodds, Norma Shelton, Richard Peterson, Russ Bryant, Russell C. Smith, Tasha Rae, my Twisted Trippin' Sistahs, and Warren Elder.

Finally, to the Rev. Michael Bernard Beckwith, founder and director of the Agape Spiritual Center in California, my gratitude for your contribution to my "soulular evolution" is immense.

Writing a book can be a solitary experience. Who would have thought that I'd have so many people to thank? If I missed anyone, please know that I count you in my blessings.

Notes

1. Eldon Taylor, *Choices and Illusions: How Did I Get Where I Am, and How Do I Get Where I Want To Be?* (Carlsbad, Calif.: Hay House, 2007), 1.

2. B. Libet, W.W. Alberts, and E. W. Wright, "Responses of Human Somatosensory Cortex to Stimuli Below Threshold for Conscious Sensation," *Science* 158 (1976): 1597–1600.

Meet Kelly McCormick

If you find yourself searching for a seat in one of Kelly McCormick's standing-room-only training seminars or keynote addresses, you might wonder what all the buzz is about. In fact, you'll be surrounded by other professionals hungry to hear Kelly's fresh and authoritative take on what's possible for themselves, their businesses, and their industries.

Rather than overloading you with heavy sales jargon or inspirational slogans, Kelly shares critical insights into human dynamics. She follows that up with her real-world business solutions and "aha" moments laced with humor.

Through the laughter and murmurs of agreement, you'll have a great time getting to know Kelly as a person. You might hear the story of her entrepreneurial prowess as a woman making inroads in fields dominated by men: owner of three successful businesses—the first by age 21—all begun during economic downturns.

And you'll likely appreciate the depth and diversity of her professional experience as an internationally respected speaker, consultant, and coach to thousands. As a former president of the Toronto Chapter of the Canadian Association of Professional Speakers and member of the National Speakers Association,

Kelly has delivered her results-driven message to all levels of retail, wholesale, commercial, corporate, franchise, association, independent business, and supply chain operations. In that sea of faces you'll find CEOs, company presidents, board members, sales professionals of all levels, customer service reps, entrepreneurs, consultants, and more.

You'll soon discover that through personal determination and perpetual improvement, Kelly has reinvented business and sales models that sorely needed to change. In place of the hard-sell, price-driven, sometimes sleazy sales world of yesterday, Kelly has brought relational and collaborative selling into the twenty-first century. She has a deep understanding of human mindsets and of the differences between men and women. Using this information, she's made it possible to personalize the sales conversation in a way that instantly connects you with your customers. In short, she shows you how to work with your buyers to find the perfect solutions they need.

Kelly's articles are widely published in print and online, including an online column for the former *Sales and Marketing Management* magazine. Her website, www.OutSellYourself.com, is loaded with tips and solutions, as well as more information about Kelly. And of course, this book, the first in the OutSell Yourself series, lays out both her story and her groundbreaking approach to business success.

Getting to know Kelly and her solutions is really an opportunity to get to know yourself and your customers in an immediate and exciting new way. It's a career-building, bottom-line-boosting opportunity for success.

Even More Resources to OutSell Yourself

1. Keep on learning.
Read reprints and excerpts from my OutSell Yourself articles on topics ranging from how to sell to women and men and how to break through tough-to-solve sales problems and challenges. Go to www.OutSellYourself.com.

2. Stay connected.
Become part of the OutSell Yourself community.
Receive just-in-time tips and resources via
Twitter at twitter.com/KellyMcCormick_, and on
Facebook at facebook.com/OutSellYourself.
And please feel free to share your thoughts about the book with the hashtag #outsellyourself on facebook.com, linkedin.com, twitter.com, goodreads.com, or any of your other favorite social networks!

3. Increase your knowledge.
Have free OutSell Yourself E-tips and blog postings sent directly to your e-mail inbox. Sign-up at www.OutSellYourself.com.

4. Get ongoing support.
Take your sales and business to the next level with one-on-one and group coaching. For a consultation to determine your goals, e-mail info@OutSellYourself.com.

5. Strengthen business and company sales.
Find out about my keynote presentations, seminars, and tele-classes at www.OutSellYourself.com. To book me to speak to your group or company, call us at 1-800-889-9637.

6. Power up your media.
For all media requests, including having me write an article for your publication, call us at 1-800-889-9637.

BONUS
FREE OutSell Yourself Bonus Tips

As an added bonus, you can download a special sales tip sheet at www.OutSellYourself.com/Bonus. It solves three of the top sales challenges for you!

Within seconds you'll find out how to:

1. **Read and Respond to Unspoken Objections** communicated through a buyer's body language
2. **Deal with Super-Agreeable People** who can't or won't make a decision
3. **Find Out How to Say "No"** when someone wants more than you want to give or are able to give

To download your FREE OutSell Yourself Bonus Tips go to: www.OutSellYourSelf.com/Bonus

Made in the USA
San Bernardino, CA
18 November 2012